Eat More
DESSERT

MORE THAN 100 SIMPLE-TO-MAKE & FUN-TO-EAT BAKED GOODS
FROM THE BAKER TO THE STARS

Jenny Keller

CREATOR OF JENNYCOOKIES.COM

PAGE STREET
PUBLISHING CO.

PAGE STREET
PUBLISHING CO.

First published in 2014 by
Page Street Publishing Co.
27 Congress Street, Suite 105
Salem, MA 01970
www.pagestreetpublishing.com

Distributed by Macmillan; sales in Canada by The Canadian Manda Group.

21   20   19   18   17   1   2   3   4   5

ISBN-13: 978-1-62414-475-2
ISBN-10: 1-62414-475-6

Library of Congress Control Number: 2017942623

Cover and book design by Page Street Publishing Co.
Photography by KCB Photography

Printed and bound in China

Page Street is proud to be a member of 1% for the Planet. Members donate one percent of their sales to one or more of the over 1,500 environmental and sustainability charities across the globe who participate in this program.

Dedication

To my sweet children, Ally and Hudson

Contents

INTRODUCTION / 6

CHAPTER 1

The Basics / 8

CHAPTER 2

Princess Tea Party / 26

CHAPTER 3

Love Is Sweet / 46

CHAPTER 4

Vintage Baby / 66

CHAPTER 5

Spring Garden / 80

CHAPTER 6

Ice Cream Shop / 104

CHAPTER 7

Down on the Farm / 124

CHAPTER 8

Shipwrecked / 142

CHAPTER 9

Campout / 158

CHAPTER 10

Fall Bounty / 178

CHAPTER 11

North Pole Bakery / 196

GLOSSARY / 219

ACKNOWLEDGMENTS / 220

ABOUT THE AUTHOR / 221

INDEX / 222

Introduction

AS I STEERED A RENTED YUKON BRIMMING WITH FRAGILE COOKIES, CUPCAKES, CAKES AND CAKE POPS THROUGH LOS ANGELES, I MARVELED AT HOW QUICKLY MY LIFE HAD CHANGED. I WAS JUST ANOTHER MOM, HAPPILY LIVING WITH MY HUSBAND AND TWO KIDS IN A SEATTLE SUBURB. IN MY SPARE TIME, I LOVED STRETCHING MY CREATIVE MUSCLES BY PUTTING TOGETHER DESSERT TABLES. THERE WAS SOMETHING INCREDIBLY FULFILLING ABOUT CREATING THEMED TABLES OF SWEET TREATS FOR MY CHILDREN'S BIRTHDAY PARTIES AND HOLIDAYS. I PICKED UP BAKING ASSIGNMENTS FROM PEOPLE WHO HEARD ABOUT MY DESSERT TABLES FROM FRIENDS HERE, OR MADE A WEDDING CAKE THERE. BUT NOW HERE I WAS, DRIVING A TRUCK FULL OF DESSERTS TO TORI SPELLING'S HOUSE FOR A BOOK PHOTO SHOOT—ALL BECAUSE OF A COOKIE.

When my beautiful daughter, Ally, was born, I fell deep under the spell that only a new baby can cast. Suddenly the coffee shop my husband, Dan, and I owned wasn't my first priority. Six months after Ally was born, my husband and I sold our business so that I could stay home. But, before long, the entrepreneur in me found the daily grind of baths, laundry, grocery shopping and dinner planning a bit boring. I needed a creative outlet to prevent myself from losing "Jenny Keller" to "Ally's Mommy."

In October 2006, Dan handed me a cookbook called *The Greatest Sugar Cookies Ever*. He loved baking with his mom when he was growing up and thought it might be something fun for Ally and I to do together. Granted, baby Ally was only ten months old at the time. Still, she could definitely monitor the sugar-cookie-baking from her high chair. So, a few days later, we gave "the greatest sugar cookies ever" a shot. Being a self-taught baker—let's just say these were *not* the greatest sugar cookies ever.

With sugar cookies on the brain, I asked my mother-in-law for her time-tested recipe. These actually were the greatest sugar cookies ever—melt-in-your-mouth soft. In no time, I was a woman obsessed. That October, I baked dozens of my version of the family recipe and created pumpkin-shaped sugar cookies, handing them out to family and friends. They were a hit.

Two weeks after Christmas, my sweet baby girl turned one. Ally was fascinated with Baby Einstein, so I built her birthday party around that theme. In preparation, I bought every Baby Einstein character I could find, gathered every ounce of primary-colored party loot, and found someone who could make custom Baby Einstein candy bar wrappers. Without realizing it, I had created my first dessert table—and it turned out that cobbling these elements together in a vibrant way was just as much fun as baking.

After that, I was constantly on the prowl for an excuse to bake themed desserts. The sugar cookies were joined by cupcakes, cakes, and cake pops—the newest dessert on the scene at the time. But, even with these additions to my repertoire, my decorated sugar cookies were still everyone's favorite. My family and friends began to affectionately call them "Jenny Cookies." I started a blog called "The Story of Us," which documented our little family's day-to-day activities, outings and milestones. Not surprisingly, pictures of my cookies and desserts overtook everything else and soon required their own blog. The Jenny Cookies blog was born.

As the months passed, the parties got more extravagant, and dessert tables became my signature. I scoured flea markets and estate sales, antique shops and secondhand stores for clever props. And I took it upon myself to ensure that every single holiday, big or small, made an impression on my kids.

St. Patrick's Day means green beer for most people, but Ally and her brother, Hudson, spent it in the park, eating shamrock-shaped sugar cookies, rainbow cupcakes and cake pops placed in a bed of Lucky Charms, while searching for a hidden pot of gold treasure. Halloween wasn't just trick-or-treating around the neighborhood; it meant inviting our closest friends and family for a celebration centered around caramel apples, caramel corn, pumpkin-shaped cake pops and cake with fondant spiders dangling from the sides. Rather than battling it out with the older kids at the local Easter Egg hunt, we had friends over to dye eggs while nibbling Easter basket cupcakes and egg-shaped sugar cookies.

The kids had a blast at these parties, but I'm not sure they had half as much fun enjoying them as I did creating them. I got a rush of excitement every time Target or Michael's set up a new display—it meant another holiday was just around the corner. I started stashing away Rubbermaid containers with goodies and supplies for future parties, just in case I needed to throw an end-of-summer campout or back-to-school bash. Of course, neither of my kids were actually in school yet, but, hey—it's always good to be prepared.

When I wasn't plotting my next party, I began taking custom orders. My "clients" consisted of friends and friends of friends, people who tasted my sugar cookies at a friend's baby shower or who sampled a cake pop at a child's birthday party. The orders were small: a few sugar cookie orders or a few dozen cupcakes. I had no intention of marketing myself as a baker, but I loved making these creative little treats, so I obliged whenever someone asked.

Then, a funny thing happened: More and more people began reading my blog and following my Jenny Cookies Facebook page. My children's parties were featured on top party sites like Amy Atlas, Kara's Party Ideas and Hostess with the Mostess. All of these posts linked to my little blog, and an unexpected viral cycle began. With more publicity came more orders. I began making cookies and dessert tables for major corporations such as JC Penney, Microsoft and Neiman Marcus. Based on demand, I started teaching occasional sold-out classes, demonstrating how to make and design Jenny Cookies. Every now and then, I considered opening a shop. But the truth is, I didn't want to go into business. I wanted to be a stay-at-home-mom and make my confections on my own time. I wanted to have my cookie and eat it, too.

Then, in 2010, my friend Kennedi attended a signing for Tori Spelling's latest book, where she gave the actress some of my cookies. Ten minutes after receiving them, Tori tweeted to thank me for the cookies. I couldn't believe it. A couple of weeks later, Tori asked if I'd make a dessert table for her party-planning book, *celebraTORI*. And, just like that, I had my first celebrity client.

With a couple of days notice, I did as much preparation for the dessert table book shoot at Tori's house as I could. Running on almost no sleep, I arrived in Los Angeles from Seattle with a suitcase full of painstakingly packed cookies and supplies. I sped to the local Target to buy a Kitchen-Aid. Once back in the house I had rented, I put the mixer to immediate use, making cakes, cake pops and even more cookies until the wee hours. Harried, I had an impromptu meeting with Tori the next day to pick out a desk, chairs and chalkboards to stage the dessert table with a classroom theme. Then it was back to my little kitchen to decorate and bake some more. I finished at 7 a.m., and within the hour I was packing up the Yukon for the shoot.

My dessert tables were featured in *celebraTORI*. Before long, I was doing dessert tables for other celebrities, including Tiffani Thiessen, Lisa Rinna and Harry Hamlin, *The Bachelorette*'s Trista Sutter and *The Bachelor*'s Jason Mesnick. My dessert tables were requested at the Emmy Awards and featured in magazines.

Although my unexpected business blossomed in ways I never expected, a lot remains the same. I bake in my home kitchen, with kids running around. I still consider myself a mom first and a baker second. And, most of all, more than fifty thousand cookies and hundreds of dessert tables later, I still get a thrill every time an idea for the next creation pops into my head.

HOW TO USE THIS BOOK

I specialize in themed dessert tables—birthdays, baby showers, weddings, you name it. I believe the dessert table is the centerpiece of any party. This book is arranged in order of parties for special occasions, holidays and for each season. But don't let the themed tables in these chapters hold you back. My desserts are mix-and-match; almost every dessert can be used for another occasion or season. Just change the color of the icing, tweak the flavors, or choose a different cake topper or decoration.

You can use this book by picking and choosing one recipe—or more!—from every chapter for your very own dessert party, or you can make all the recipes in your favorite chapter to create a beautiful dessert table.

1

The Basics

THESE CORE RECIPES ARE REPLICATED AND REPRODUCED THROUGHOUT MY
DESSERT TABLES BY TWEAKING FLAVORS OR SWAPPING DECORATING TECHNIQUES.

Buttercream Frosting Recipe

YEARS BACK, I SENT MY HUSBAND TO THE STORE FOR A FEW GROCERIES. ON THE LIST WAS MARGARINE. HE CAME BACK WITH THE STORE BRAND. ASSUMING THAT IT DIDN'T MATTER, I MADE MY BUTTERCREAM FROSTING. UNFORTUNATELY, THE OFF-BRAND MARGARINE COLORED MY ICING YELLOW. BECAUSE OF THIS, I'M A STICKLER FOR IMPERIAL BRAND MARGARINE. IT'S THE LIGHTEST SHADE OF MARGARINE, WHICH PREVENTS MY ICING FROM BECOMING A COLOR BEFORE I'VE COLORED IT.

IT'S TYPICALLY MADE FROM MILK, BUTTER AND CONFECTIONERS' SUGAR. ALTHOUGH NOT TRUE "BUTTERCREAM" IN THE SENSE THAT MY FROSTING RECIPE HAS NO ACTUAL BUTTER IN IT, I LOVE THAT MINE SPREADS AND TASTES BETTER WHEN MADE WITH IMPERIAL MARGARINE AND CRISCO SHORTENING. I THINK YOU'LL LOVE IT, TOO.

THIS BASIC BUTTERCREAM FROSTING WORKS FOR A VARIETY OF PURPOSES. DEPENDING ON WHICH DESSERT YOU'RE MAKING, MY BASIC BUTTERCREAM RECIPE MAY BE TWEAKED. ADD COCOA POWDER FOR A CHOCOLATE FROSTING OR DROP IN SOME PEPPERMINT OR LEMON EXTRACT TO PUMP UP THE FLAVOR. IF YOU LIVE IN A WARM CLIMATE, IT'S A GOOD IDEA TO USE HALF THE MILK ADDED TO THE BUTTERCREAM RECIPE SO THE ICING IS FIRMER. IT'S VERY FLUFFY AND MELTS EASILY IN WARM WEATHER.

MAKES ABOUT 6 CUPS

INGREDIENTS

1 CUP (225 G) IMPERIAL MARGARINE OR BUTTER (2 STICKS)

1 CUP (225 G) CRISCO VEGETABLE SHORTENING

2 POUNDS (907 G) CONFECTIONERS' SUGAR (ABOUT 7½ CUPS)

2 TEASPOONS PURE VANILLA EXTRACT

3 TABLESPOONS (45 ML) WHOLE MILK

DIRECTIONS

1. Combine the margarine and Crisco in the bowl of an electric mixer; using a paddle attachment, beat on medium speed until smooth, about 2 minutes.

2. Add half of the confectioners' sugar and continue beating on low speed for an additional 2 minutes, or until the mixture is creamy, scraping the sides of the bowl with a rubber spatula as needed. Add the remaining confectioners' sugar, vanilla and milk, and beat until the frosting is creamy and fluffy, about 2 minutes more. Add any food coloring at this time, if using, and beat on low speed until light and fluffy.

3. Use immediately or store in an airtight container refrigerated for up to 30 days.

BUTTERCREAM TIPS

♥   I use AmeriColor soft gel paste in squeeze bottles, found at most baking stores, because the colors are so vibrant and the tiniest bit goes a long way. Some colors are much stronger than others. Like paint drying, pink tends to get darker as the frosting dries. In this case, less is more.

♥   Other recipes call for deep, darker colors like red, black, and brown. For these colors, you need to use a lot more to get the rich shades you desire. Start off with a little and add more as needed. If you add too much gel at first, you can always mix in more frosting to lighten the color in the bowl.

Chocolate Buttercream Frosting

MAKES ABOUT 6 CUPS

INGREDIENTS

1 CUP (225 G) IMPERIAL MARGARINE (2 STICKS)

1 CUP (225 G) CRISCO VEGETABLE SHORTENING

1 CUP (118 G) UNSWEETENED COCOA POWDER

2 POUNDS (907 G) CONFECTIONERS' SUGAR (ABOUT 7½ CUPS)

2 TEASPOONS PURE VANILLA EXTRACT

4 TO 6 TABLESPOONS (60-90 ML) WHOLE MILK, AS NEEDED

DIRECTIONS

1. Combine the margarine and Crisco in the bowl of an electric mixer and beat on medium speed until smooth, about 2 minutes.

2. Whisk the cocoa powder and confectioners' sugar together in a large bowl. Add half of the dry ingredients to the margarine mixture and continue beating on low speed until the mixture is creamy, about 2 minutes. Add the remaining dry ingredients, vanilla and milk, and beat until the frosting is light and fluffy, about 2 to 3 minutes more.

3. Use immediately or store in an airtight container refrigerated for up to 30 days.

Sugar Cookies

This is the recipe that started it all and the one that will always be dearest to me. Every time I tell students in my cookie decorating class that these sugar cookies are fail-proof, they eye me suspiciously. But once they try it themselves, they agree: Anyone can make them, and everyone will love them.

Makes about 24 cookies

INGREDIENTS

3 CUPS (375 G) ALL-PURPOSE FLOUR, PLUS MORE FOR ROLLING

2 TEASPOON ALUMINUM-FREE BAKING POWDER

1 CUP (225 G) SALTED BUTTER (2 STICKS), AT ROOM TEMPERATURE (DO NOT USE MARGARINE FOR THIS RECIPE; IT TASTES BETTER WITH BUTTER)

1 CUP (200 G) GRANULATED SUGAR

1 LARGE EGG

2 TEASPOONS PURE VANILLA EXTRACT

1 BATCH BUTTERCREAM FROSTING (PAGE 10)

DIRECTIONS

1. Into a medium bowl, combine the flour and baking powder with a whisk. Set aside.

2. In a large bowl, using an electric mixer fitted with the paddle attachment on medium speed, beat the butter and sugar for about 1½ minutes, or until smooth. Beat in the egg and vanilla until well combined. Scrape the sides of the bowl with a rubber spatula.

3. Turn the mixer speed to low and carefully add the flour mixture a little at a time, occasionally stopping to scrape the sides of the bowl. Once all the flour has been incorporated, the dough should form a ball around the mixing attachment and feel soft but not sticky.

4. Wrap the dough ball in a piece of plastic wrap and press down to form a 1-inch (2.5 cm)-thick disk. Refrigerate for at least 10 minutes before rolling or store for up to 7 days tightly wrapped.

5. Preheat the oven to 375°F (190°C).

6. Roll out the dough on a lightly floured flat work surface to about ¼-inch (6 mm) thickness, using additional flour as necessary to prevent sticking. Use cookie cutters to create desired shapes, and carefully transfer with a cookie spatula to a nonstick baking sheet, placing the cookies about ¾ inch (2 cm) apart.

7. Bake one sheet at a time in the middle of the oven for about 7-8 minutes, or until puffy. Allow the cookies to rest for 2 minutes on the baking sheet before transferring to a wire rack to cool completely.

8. Continue rolling out the gathered scraps and remaining disk until all the dough has been used.

9. Decorate the cookies with my buttercream frosting.

While I'm waiting for my dough to chill in the refrigerator, I always regroup my kitchen. If you've ever been to my house, you'll notice I'm constantly picking up. I have a hard time sitting down to relax if there's a sink full of dishes. So when I'm baking, I clean as I go. Baking's less stressful when you have a clean countertop to work from.

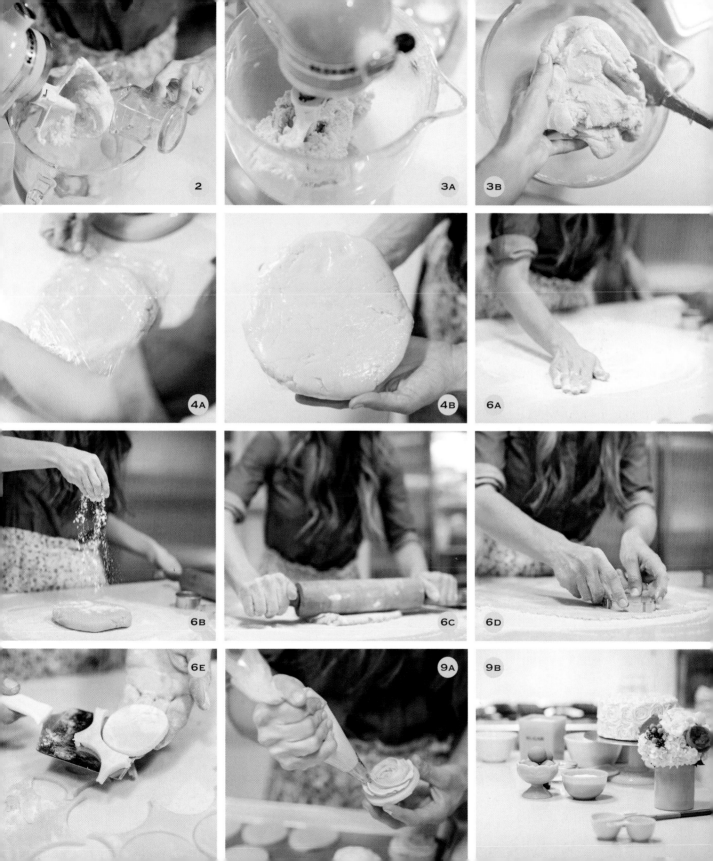

COOKIE-MAKING TIPS

- ♥ For best taste and results, I only use real butter in my cookies.

- ♥ Because some ovens are finicky due to "hot spots" and uneven temperatures, baking one sheet at a time on the middle rack ensures the cookies have a better chance of baking evenly.

- ♥ If you're feeling adventurous, you can add food coloring to your cookie dough for colored sugar cookies. Fall leaf and spring flower cookies look great with food coloring.

- ♥ I try to keep my cookie decorating designs minimal. Rather than pipe on every last detail of a cookie (faces, names, extreme details), keep it simple. All those extra details can make your cookie look overdecorated and messy. In addition to standard round tips, I often use star tips that create texture (shown in wedding dress, heart, sheep, ice cream cone and pine cone cookies).

SOURCING COOKIE CUTTERS

Over the years, I've become a cookie cutter collector. I've learned the hard way that if I see one I like, I should grab it, even if I don't have an immediate use for it—especially since they tend to be $1 or less. They always come in handy down the line (and sometimes, one cookie cutter can trigger an entire dessert table theme). My go-to spots for cookie cutters are Wilton.com, Thecookiecuttershop.com, Michael's and JoAnn Fabric & Crafts.

Basic Cake Recipe

I'M ALL ABOUT MAKING THINGS EASY IN THE KITCHEN, SO I USE LOTS OF CAKE MIXES IN ASSORTED FLAVORS TO SUIT THE OCCASION. YOU CAN USE CAKE MIXES FOR CAKE LAYERS, CUPCAKES AND AS THE BASE FOR MY CAKE POPS. ALTHOUGH DUNCAN HINES IS MY FAVORITE BRAND BECAUSE IT'S SO MOIST AND RICH, ANY QUALITY CAKE MIX WILL DO. AND BECAUSE I LOVE MOIST CAKE, I ALMOST ALWAYS ADD AN EXTRA EGG AND A BOX OF INSTANT PUDDING TO THE BATTER.

MAKES TWO STANDARD 8-INCH (20.5 CM) ROUND CAKES OR TWO DOZEN CUPCAKES.

INGREDIENTS

COOKING SPRAY OR CRISCO OR BUTTER PLUS FLOUR, FOR PANS

1 (18.25-OUNCE [517 G]) BOX DUNCAN HINES CAKE MIX (USE YOUR FAVORITE CAKE FLAVOR)

1 (3.4-OUNCE [110 G]) BOX JELL-O INSTANT PUDDING AND PIE FILLING, DRY (USE A FLAVOR TO COMPLEMENT THE CAKE MIX)

1 CUP (235 ML) WATER

⅓ CUP (80 ML) OIL

4 LARGE EGGS

DIRECTIONS

1. Preheat the oven to 350°F (180°C). Coat two 8-inch (20.5 cm) round nonstick cake pans with cooking spray, or grease and flour the pans, tapping out the excess flour. Set the prepared pans aside.

2. In a large bowl, and using an electric stand mixer fitted with a paddle attachment, beat the cake mix, pudding mix, water, oil and eggs on medium speed for 2 to 3 minutes, or until well blended. Scrape the sides of the bowl and mix again until all the ingredients are incorporated.

3. Pour the batter into the prepared cake pans, filling each one approximately three-quarters full.

4. Place the pans in the preheated oven, on middle rack. Bake the cakes for 30 to 35 minutes, or until a toothpick inserted into the center comes out clean.

5. Remove the pans from the oven and place on wire cooling racks for 25 to 30 minutes.

6. Run a knife around the edges of the cakes, flip the pans over, and gently extract the cakes.

7. Return the cakes to the wire racks and finish cooling completely before frosting and decorating.

8. After the layers are cooled, freeze or refrigerate the cakes for 1 hour before decorating, to reduce crumbs and make for a smoother icing process. Decorate as directed.

CAKE-BAKING AND DECORATING TIPS

When I was in college, I'd make cakes in a 9" × 13" (23 × 33 cm) pan, ice it with canned frosting, and call it good. While it may have tasted good (to a college kid), those cakes had zero presentation. Cakes are the centerpiece of a dessert table. They stand tall and pull the table together like little pieces of art. These days, I have even less free time than I had in college, so I'm always thinking of new ways to pull off a gorgeous cake in a flash.

BAKING THE CAKE

♥ I use Duncan Hines cake mixes as the foundation of my cakes; they're moist and rich. Just a few additional ingredients pump up the flavor and enhance the cake's texture. Change your frosting and filling options to mix it up.

♥ It's an ugly thing to see cake crumbs scattered through your white creamy frosting, so prepare your cake pans before diving into the cake batter. I spray or grease my cake pans first, then add 1 to 2 teaspoons of flour to the pan and coat the sides and bottoms, tapping out the excess flour when done. This way, the cake is less likely to stick and rip the cake bottoms to shreds.

♥ All ovens are not created equal: Once in a while, you should check your oven's temperature with an oven thermometer to be sure it's holding an even heat. If it's not, you can recalibrate the temperature, and you should be good to go again.

♥ Check the cake layers and cupcakes for doneness by inserting a toothpick or cake tester into the center. If it comes out clean with no gooey batter, the cake's done. Remove from the oven right away.

DECORATING THE CAKE

♥ I love textured buttercream-frosted cakes. They're quick to decorate and gorgeous to look at. Roses, ribbons, swirls and scallops give your cake a timeless look in minutes. Mix shredded coconut, nuts and even chocolate chips into my basic buttercream (page 10) for additional texture variety.

♥ When they come out of the oven, place the pans on wire cooling racks and let sit for 15 or more minutes. At that point, it should be safe to remove the layers from their pans. Let cool completely and chill or freeze for at least an hour before decorating with frosting.

♥ When it's time to decorate, you may need to trim the tops of the layers to make them flat. You don't want a big bulge in the middle of your cake. You'll also need to take a few minutes to "crumb coat" your cake so you won't have all those ugly crumbs showing.

♥ Use an angled cake spatula to cover the cake completely with a very thin layer of icing (or crumb coat) to help reduce the amount of crumbs in the final coat of icing. Then it's time to finish decorating your masterpiece.

♥ **Petal cake:** Wilton tip 2D
♥ **Ribbon cake:** Wilton tip 104 (or any petal tip, depending on how large you want your "ribbons")
♥ **Rose cake:** Wilton tip 1M or any large closed star tip
♥ **Ruffle cake:** Wilton tips 103 or 104 (or any petal tip, depending on how large you want your "ruffles")
♥ **Rustic cake:** use pointed angle spatula to create layers of ridged buttercream
♥ **Scalloped cake:** Wilton tip 10 and angled spatula
♥ **Spackle cake:** smear icing to resemble spackle by using Wilton cupcake spatula

Basic Cupcake Recipe

JUST AS FOR MY CAKES, I USE A CAKE MIX BASE FOR MY CUPCAKES. WHILE I LOVE THE CLASSIC FLAVORS, SOMETIMES I ADD FUN EXTRAS TO SPICE THEM UP. CHOPPED CANDY BARS, SMALL COOKIES, NUTS AND HINTS OF FLAVORED EXTRACTS GIVE CUPCAKES THAT EXTRA FLAIR WHEN YOU WANT SOMETHING MORE THAN A BASIC WHITE OR CHOCOLATE CAKE.

MAKES 24 CUPCAKES

INGREDIENTS

(PAGE 15)

DIRECTIONS

1. Follow the directions for the batter for the Basic Cake recipe, making the following changes.

2. Using a cookie scoop, add one scoop of batter into each cupcake liner to create a batch of perfectly even cupcakes.

3. Bake the cupcakes at 350°F (180°C) for 18 to 20 minutes, or until a wooden toothpick can be inserted and cleanly removed. Remove the cupcakes from the oven and place the tray on a wire cooling rack for 15 minutes.

4. Take the cupcakes out of the tray and allow them to cool completely on the cooling racks before decorating.

Cupcake Baking Tips

♥ Using a medium-size cookie scoop is an easy way to deposit the cake batter into the cupcake tins. For best results, fill the cups 2 two-thirds full with batter, unless the cupcakes require additional fillings.

♥ Because most ovens bake differently and often have "hot spots," it's best to rotate the pans halfway through baking. Turn the pans once and switch places from top to bottom racks.

♥ Standard and mini cupcakes require different baking times. Cupcakes are done when a toothpick inserted into the center comes out clean.

Cupcake Decorating Tips

There are so many ways to dress these little cakes, from assorted buttercream decorating techniques, to topping them with candy molded shapes. Dip them in a bowl of sparkling sanding sugar or sprinkle with a few colored sprinkles.

♥ Candy molds are widely available in just about any shape imaginable. When I haven't been able to source a particular shape, I've found various molds used for clay, soap and fondant making on etsy.com.

♥ Basic swirl: Wilton tip 1M (starting from outside and working your way in)

♥ Standard: Wilton round tip 1A or 2A, Ateco 800 or 804

♥ Rose: use tip 1M (starting from inside working your way out)

♥ Ruffle: use tip 104 (or any petal tip you like depending on how large you want your "ruffle")

♥ Hydrangea: Wilton tip 2D

♥ Star Swirl: Ateco tip 869

Cake Pops

A CAKE POP IS A FORM OF CAKE DISGUISED AS A LOLLIPOP. CAKE CRUMBS ARE MIXED WITH ICING AND FORMED INTO A BALL, THEN ATTACHED TO A LOLLIPOP STICK AND DIPPED IN CANDY MELTS.

THE FIRST TIME I TRIED {CAKE POP QUEEN} BAKERELLA'S RED VELVET CAKE POP RECIPE, I SWORE I'D NEVER DO IT AGAIN. MY HANDS WERE TOO STICKY TO ROLL THE BALLS, NOT TO MENTION THEY TURNED BRIGHT RED. WHEN I FINALLY FORMED ENOUGH BALLS TO DIP, THE MELTED CANDY LOOKED CLUMPY AND THE BALLS KEPT FALLING OFF MY STICKS.

THEN I GOT A CALL FROM THE EVERETT CLINIC, A HUGE MEDICAL PRACTICE IN MY AREA. THEY WERE BEING NAMED ONE OF THE BEST COMPANIES TO WORK FOR IN WASHINGTON STATE AND WANTED 1,725 CAKE POPS TO CELEBRATE. I JUST ABOUT DIED: 1725? WAS THAT EVEN POSSIBLE? OF COURSE I SAID YES.

AS WITH EVERYTHING IN LIFE, PRACTICE MAKES PERFECT. YOU DON'T NEED TO MAKE 1,725 BEFORE YOU NAIL THE RECIPE, BUT GIVE THESE CAKE POPS A COUPLE TRIES BEFORE GIVING UP.

MAKES 40 POPS

INGREDIENTS

1 (18.25-OUNCE [517 G]) BOX DUNCAN HINES CAKE MIX (USE YOUR FAVORITE CAKE FLAVOR)

1 (3.4-OUNCE [110 G]) BOX JELL-O INSTANT PUDDING AND PIE FILLING, DRY (USE A FLAVOR TO COMPLEMENT THE CAKE MIX)

1 CUP (235 ML) WATER

⅓ CUP (80 ML) OIL

4 LARGE EGGS

½ TO ¾ CUP (120 TO 175 ML) BUTTERCREAM ICING (PAGE 10) OR CANNED ICING IN YOUR CHOICE OF FLAVOR

3 (12-OUNCE [340G]) PACKAGES CANDY MELTS, YOUR CHOICE OF COLOR

DECORATIONS, SPRINKLES, CHOPPED NUTS, ETC.

YOU WILL NEED

40 LOLLIPOP STICKS

DIRECTIONS

1. Preheat the oven to 350°F (180°C). Coat a 9 × 13-inch (23 × 33 cm) baking pan with cooking spray, or grease and flour pan, tapping out excess flour. Set aside.

2. In a large bowl, and using an electric stand mixer fitted with a paddle attachment, beat the cake mix, pudding mix, water, oil and eggs on medium speed for 2 to 3 minutes, or until well blended. Scrape the sides of the bowl and mix again until all the ingredients are incorporated.

3. Likewise, if making brownies, follow the directions on the box of brownie mix.

4. Pour the batter into the prepared cake pan. Place the pan in the preheated oven, and bake for 35 to 40 minutes, or until a toothpick inserted into the center comes out clean.

5. Remove the pan from the oven and place on a wire cooling rack for 25 to 30 minutes. Let cool completely before making cake pops.

6. Mash up the cake and place in a large bowl. Using an electric stand mixer fitted with a paddle attachment, mix cake and ½ to ¾ cup (120 to 175 ml) of icing on medium speed until moist and well blended and mixture can be molded into a ball.

7. Measure and roll mixture into 1 tablespoon-size balls, and place on a cookie sheet. Refrigerate for 1 hour or until firm.

8. Melt the candy melts in separate microwave-safe bowls in 30-second increments at 40% power for about 2 to 3 minutes, stirring as needed until smooth.

9. Remove the pops from the refrigerator. Dip each lollipop stick ¼ inch (6 mm) into the melted candy. Insert the sticks into all the cake balls. (The melted candy will adhere the lollipop sticks to the cake balls to prevent them from falling off the sticks when dipping).

10. Proceed by dipping the entire cake ball down into the melted candy. Lightly sprinkle each with the decorations of your choice while the candy is still tacky. Stand the pops up in a sheet of Styrofoam to dry.

CAKE POP TIPS

♥ Mash the baked cake (or brownies) with your hands to break it up first, then continue mixing with a stand mixer.

♥ Begin by adding ½ cup (120 ml) of buttercream frosting to the cake. If it doesn't hold together to make a ball, add another ¼ cup (60 ml) of frosting. Some cake pops take more than others.

♥ A tablespoon-size cookie scoop is a handy gadget to keep all your cake pops the same size. You can also measure the dough with a standard tablespoon. Roll the balls by hand to make them perfectly round.

♥ When dipping cake pops in the melted candy, use a deep bowl. Dip the balls completely, making sure to cover the first ¼ inch (6 mm) of the lollipop stick. This ensures that the pops stay on the sticks.

♥ Add a bit of vegetable oil to your candy melts if they're too thick for dipping.

♥ Have a piece of Styrofoam ready to stick the cake pops in to dry.

Rice Krispie Treats

LIKE SUGAR COOKIES AND BROWNIES, THIS
SWEET LITTLE TREAT CAN BECOME JUST ABOUT
ANYTHING—CHRISTMAS TREES, FLOWERS,
PUMPKINS, YOU NAME IT.

MAKES 24 TREATS

INGREDIENTS

3 TABLESPOONS (42 G) BUTTER OR MARGARINE

1 (10-OUNCE [280 G]) PACKAGE
MINI MARSHMALLOWS (4 CUPS)

6 CUPS (150 G) RICE KRISPIES CEREAL

DIRECTIONS

1. Lightly oil a spray a 9 × 13-inch (23 × 33 cm) baking pan
with vegetable spray.

2. In a large saucepan over low heat, melt butter or margarine.
Add the marshmallows and stir until melted and smooth. Remove
the pan from the heat and add any food coloring at this time.

3. Add the Rice Krispies and stir until completely coated. Pat into
the prepared baking pan and let cool completely to set. Once set,
cut out desired shapes, using cookie cutters.

RICE KRISPIE TIPS

♥ Color it: With just a few drops of food coloring, this treat
can morph into any color you wish.

♥ Cut it: Using a cookie cutter, cut it into a shape that
perfectly suits your party theme.

♥ Dip it: Dip it in candy melts to add an extra coat of
flavor. Place it on a lollipop stick and turn it into a pop.

♥ Mold it: Shape your treats into pumpkins, Easter eggs,
sports balls, ornaments, baby rattles and more.

ESSENTIAL INGREDIENTS

These simple ingredients are easy to find at any grocery store.
They're used in many of my recipes.

♥ **Cake mix:** You can use any good cake mix, but I prefer Duncan
Hines because it's moist and rich.

♥ **Butter or margarine:** I love using Imperial margarine for my
buttercream frosting (page 10) because I think it tastes better
and produces smoother frosting. That said, I only use *real* butter
in my Jenny Cookies. Otherwise, they can be interchanged in
recipes like Rice Krispie treats and other homemade cookie
varieties.

♥ **Confectioners' sugar:** Also known as powdered sugar, you'll
use lots in my buttercream frosting recipe.

♥ **Vanilla and extracts:** Vanilla and all other extracts taste best
when they're pure, but imitation will also work. Any brand
will do.

♥ **Vegetable shortening:** I use Crisco solid shortening for my
buttercream frosting and love that it comes in premeasured
one-cup (225 g) sticks.

♥ **Oil:** Vegetable oil.

♥ **Flour:** I only use all-purpose flour for my Jenny Cookies.

♥ **Baking powder:** Use aluminum-free baking powder; it's better
for you.

♥ **Sugar:** Use granulated sugar, unless the recipe specifies brown
sugar, which should always be measured after it's packed in the
measuring cup.

♥ **Eggs:** For best results, I use large eggs.

♥ **Pudding:** I use JELL-O Instant Pudding and Pie Filling for all
my cakes and cupcakes.

♥ **Rice cereal:** I like to use Rice Krispies, but any crispy rice cereal
will work.

♥ **Food coloring:** AmeriColor gives my desserts and frostings the
vibrant color they deserve. Wilton colors also work.

♥ **Candy oils:** AmeriColor candy oil also works best to color
candy melts.

♥ **Candy melts:** I like the Guittard brand, which are smoothest
and easy to find online. Wilton candy melts will also work.

TOOLS OF THE TRADE

These are some of the tools, gadgets and equipment I use while baking. I'm assuming you already have a stove, oven and refrigerator in your kitchen.

- Both a heavy-duty high-speed stand mixer and a powerful hand mixer with whip and beater attachments
- Food processer for chopping nuts, chopping cookies (for cake pops) and crushing candy canes, candy bars, etc.
- Baking pans: 4-, 6-, 7-, 8-, 9-, and 10-inch (10, 15, 18, 20.5, 23, and 25.5 cm) round nonstick or silicone cake pans
- 9 × 13-inch (23 × 3 cm) Pyrex glass or metal baking pans
- Nonstick baking or cookie sheets
- Muffin pans or cupcake trays, standard and mini sizes
- Paper cupcake liners
- Wire cooling racks
- Oven thermometer
- Candy thermometer
- Sharp knives (utility and long, serrated knife for trimming cake tops)
- Rolling pin
- Mixing bowls in all sizes
- Microwave-safe bowls for melting candy melts

- Measuring cups and spoons
- Offset angled spatula for decorating
- Offset angled pointed spatula for decorating
- Straight spatula and cookie spatula
- Spatulas, either rubber or plastic
- Metal spatula for removing hot cookies from pans
- Cookie scoops, both large and small
- Plastic wrap
- Pot holders or oven mitts

DECORATIONS

You can find many decorating items and ingredients at craft stores or your local supermarket. Others are on Amazon.com or at cake-decorating websites; Wilton.com and gygi.com are two of my favorites.

- Sixlets, gumballs, M&M's, Tootsie Rolls, jelly beans
- Sprinkles, Disco Dust, sanding sugar, sugar crystals
- Popsicle and lollipop sticks, for handheld desserts
- Paper and plastic straws, for cake pops
- ¼-inch [6mm]-thick dowels and thick plastic straws, for separating and supporting cake layers
- Styrofoam, for drying cake pops
- Decorating bags, disposable and plastic
- Wilton and Ateco decorating tips in various sizes
- Wilton couplers, used with decorating tips to make switching tips easier
- Plastic bottles, for melting and squirting melted candy melts
- Candy molds, for making candy decorations
- Cookie cutters, in all shapes and sizes
- Cake boards, cardboard or plastic in various sizes for separating multitiered cakes
- Ribbon and Baker's twine, in various sizes and colors of ribbons for decorating your desserts

HOW TO CREATE THE PERFECT DESSERT TABLE

♥ **Choose a theme:** The first step in creating a fabulous dessert table is to choose a theme. I always begin with a few inspiration pieces. It may be the party invitation; a grouping of gorgeous cake plates; a decorative object; or a certain color. Gathering a few items gets the ideas flowing and creates the concept.

♥ **Choose a color:** Choosing a color palette is a must. You want your table to flow, so creating this boundary of colors helps to keep everything in check. I like to include a variety of colors in my tables. It's easy to find fun props and display pieces when you have a mixture of colors. It's nearly impossible to color coordinate everything in your dessert table when tied to one specific color.

♥ **Plan ahead:** Select your theme a couple of months in advance (if possible) to give yourself time to pick up things gradually. There's nothing worse than racing around the day before the party trying to find everything you need.

♥ **Set the table:** Whenever I create a dessert table, I begin with my display first and add the desserts once the table has been set. The first step is selecting your table and deciding whether or not you'll use a tablecloth. So many times I've searched stores for the perfect matching or coordinating party tablecloth and left disappointed and empty handed. There are only so many tablecloths out there. But fabrics—there are millions! So now, instead of heading to a department store, I head straight to the fabric store.

♥ **Use height:** This is a key element in table design. A table of various desserts scattered on a flat table does nothing for presentation—it looks like a potluck. Add height with stacked cake plates, wood crates or boxes, and then arrange your cake stands, trays and other display pieces until they look appealing.

♥ **Mix it up:** To determine which dessert to display on which plate, contrast. Don't put a pink cake on a pink cake plate if there's a mint green option. The mint green will make your pink cake pop. White desserts on white cake plates are lost (unless you want an all-white table).

♥ **Add flowers:** Add pops of flowers to fill in gaps. Not all dessert tables warrant fresh flowers, but sometimes they're the perfect way to add a bit of life to a table and fill in any holes.

♥ **Be resourceful:** Thinking outside the box when it comes to your dessert platters adds interest to your table. It's so much more fun to look at a table filled with random objects holding the dessert than a table filled with the same colored cake stand. I've used all kind of random things for my cake "stands." Galvanized buckets and apple baskets turned upside down, pieces of old scrap wooden rounds, tree stumps, tin boxes, even a vintage Christmas sled.

♥ **Love your cake:** The cake is the centerpiece of the dessert table. Cakes create a focal point no matter where they are placed on the table. They're the dessert that stands tall above the rest, so naturally they take on the centerpiece role.

♥ **Create a backdrop:** Depending on the placement of your dessert table, you may want to create a backdrop. Years ago, I picked up a big piece of plywood that I've transformed into more dessert table backdrops than I can count. All you need is a staple gun and fabric, which could be as basic as a tablecloth, sheet or even an old window panel. Staple the fabric to the plywood, and in minutes you'll have a custom backdrop. Garlands, paper flowers, paper pinwheels and bunting banners can be strung across or attached to it for added décor.

♥ **Know your audience:** Gender, age, number of guests and time of party. This will help you determine the size, quantity, variety and types of desserts to offer your guests. For example, baby shower guests are usually women, and showers typically happen in the early afternoon. Keeping that in mind, desserts should be small, bite size and snacklike. I don't know a lot of women who want to shove a regular-size cupcake in their mouth while oohing over tiny baby clothes.

♥ **Do guests a "favor":** With all the commotion at parties, it's hard to totally appreciate the dessert you are eating while trying to keep a conversation alive. Most people (especially women) would much rather take a box to go and enjoy their dessert at home. To-go containers not only double as a party favor but also guarantee you won't be left with uneaten dessert.

2

Princess Tea Party

LIKE MOST LITTLE GIRLS, MY DAUGHTER, ALLY, LOVES PRINCESSES. SO FOR HER SEVENTH BIRTHDAY, I WANTED TO THROW HER A PARTY FIT FOR A PRINCESS. MY GOAL WAS TO CONVEY THE ESSENCE OF CINDERELLA WITHOUT OVERTLY INCORPORATING HER CHARACTER INTO THE DESSERTS OR DESIGN. I WANTED ALLY'S PARTY TO LOOK CHIC RATHER THAN OVERRIDDEN WITH TRADEMARKED CHARACTERS, SO WE CHOSE A PRINCESS TEA PARTY THEME WITH OBVIOUS CINDERELLA ACCENTS.

For the princess tea party table, I began with a soft blue and pink color palette, in addition to vintage teacups and floral fabrics as my inspiration. You might notice these are the colors frequently found throughout Disney's Cinderella illustrations, particularly in Cinderella's two ball gowns. The actual desserts on the table incorporate shapes we all associate with Cinderella: The sugar cookies are shaped like carriages, shoes and crowns. Rice Krispie treats are in the shape of a magic wand. The cake is decorated simply but in dreamy textures that capture a floaty, fairy-tale essence.

Try using elements (teacups, saucers, cake stands, fabric napkins) made up of mismatched pieces that flow together to give the table an elegant, feminine and princess feel. Also use lace doilies and floral-patterned tablecloths to give the table a soft yet sweet look.

SETTING THE TABLE

Instead of creating a separate table space for your desserts, use your tea party table as your dessert table. These gorgeous miniature desserts make the perfect centerpiece for your tea party. Like the mismatched teacups and saucers, continue this look for the dessert display. Since the desserts are relatively small, you'll want to keep your display pieces to scale. Small dessert pedestals can be made by gluing glass candlesticks to tea plates (I found mine at Goodwill). A variety of vintage cake plates and compotes in assorted heights and pastel colors help to quickly and easily pull the table display together. Ribbon bows tied onto lollipop sticks and fresh rose petals placed in the bed of the Rice Krispie wands give your table sweet, feminine detail.

Everything you need for the perfect princess tea party table can be sourced from a variety of places, beginning with your own home—you'll be surprised at how many basic elements you have on hand. The extra flourishes should be easily and cheaply obtained. In this case, I also found doilies and old floral patterned sheets (repurposed as tablecloths) at Goodwill. Other items can be picked up at estate sales, flea markets, antique stores and even Grandma's attic.

PRINCESS TEA PARTY DESSERTS

- ♥ **Royal Chocolate Ruffle Cake**
- ♥ **Enchanted Rose Cupcakes**
- ♥ **Charming Chocolate Cupcake Truffles**
- ♥ **Sparkle Rice Krispie Wands**
- ♥ **Marshmallow Pillow Pops**
- ♥ **Bibbidi Bobbidi Blue Cake Pops**
- ♥ **Royal Carriage Sugar Cookies**
- ♥ **Princess Tiara Sugar Cookies**
- ♥ **Glass Slipper Sugar Cookies**
- ♥ **Magic Wand Sugar Cookies**

Royal Chocolate Ruffle Cake

THIS CAKE IS MADE DELICIOUS WITH A JAZZED-UP CAKE MIX AND DECORATED WITH MY BASIC BUTTERCREAM FROSTING. WITH THE RIGHT DECORATING TOOLS AND A FEW TWISTS OF THE WRIST, THESE CHARMING RUFFLES WILL DELIGHT ALL THE PRINCESSES AT THE PARTY. DISPLAYING IT ON A TALL FOOTED CAKE PLATE WILL ALLOW IT TO STAND HIGH ABOVE ALL THE OTHER DESSERTS ON THE TABLE AND WILL GUARANTEE PLENTY OF OOOHS AND AAHS FROM YOUR GUESTS.

MAKES ONE 6-INCH (15 CM) AND 8-INCH (20.5 CM) TIERED CAKE

INGREDIENTS

COOKING SPRAY OR CRISCO OR BUTTER PLUS FLOUR, FOR PANS

2 (18.25-OUNCE [517 G]) BOXES DUNCAN HINES DEVIL'S FOOD CAKE MIX

2 (3.4-OUNCE [110 G]) BOXES JELL-O CHOCOLATE INSTANT PUDDING AND PIE FILLING, DRY

2 CUPS (475 ML) WATER

⅔ CUP (157 ML) OIL

8 LARGE EGGS

3 BATCHES WHITE BUTTERCREAM FROSTING (PAGE 10)

DIRECTIONS

1. Preheat the oven to 350°F (180°C). Coat the two 6-inch (15 cm) and two 8-inch (20.5 cm) round nonstick cake pans with cooking spray, or grease and flour the pans, tapping out the excess flour. Set the prepared pans aside.

2. In a large bowl, and using an electric stand mixer fitted with a paddle attachment, beat the cake mix, pudding mix, water, oil and eggs on medium speed for 2 to 3 minutes, or until well blended. Scrape the sides of the bowl and mix again until all the ingredients are incorporated.

3. Pour the batter into the prepared cake pans, filling each one approximately three-quarters full.

4. Place the pans in the preheated oven, on middle rack. Bake the 6-inch (15 cm) cakes for 25 to 30 minutes, and the 8-inch (20.5 cm) cakes for 30 to 35 minutes, or until a toothpick inserted into the center comes out clean.

5. Meanwhile, make buttercream frosting, following the directions on page 10.

6. Remove the pans from the oven and place on wire cooling racks for 25 to 30 minutes. Run a knife around the edges of the cakes, flip the pans over and gently extract the cakes. Return the cakes to the wire racks and finish cooling completely before frosting and decorating. After the layers are cooled, freeze or refrigerate the cakes for 1 hour before decorating to reduce crumbs and make for a smoother icing process.

(continued)

2 (8 × 2-INCH [20.5 × 5 CM]) AND
2 (6 × 2-INCH [15 × 4 CM]) ROUND
NONSTICK CAKE PANS

CAKE CUTTER OR LONG, SERRATED
KNIFE

2 ROUND CARDBOARD OR PLASTIC
CAKE BOARDS

OFFSET ANGLED SPATULA

5 (¼-INCH [6 MM]-THICK) DOWELS OR
THICK PLASTIC STRAWS

LARGE, FLAT SPATULA

CAKE DECORATING TURNTABLE

1 LARGE PASTRY BAG

#103 WILTON DECORATING TIP

1 WILTON COUPLER

2 LOLLIPOP STICKS

FABRIC SCRAPS

BAKER'S TWINE OR BUNTING STRING

TO ASSEMBLE AND DECORATE THE CAKE

1. Before decorating, trim the crowns from the cake layer tops with a cake cutter or long, serrated knife so that they are flat and even.

2. Place one of the 8-inch (20.5 cm) cakes on a cake board. Using the angled cake spatula, spread about ½ cup (120 ml) of the buttercream frosting evenly across the top of the cake layer. Place the second 8-inch (20.5 cm) cake on top of the first, with the cut side on the bottom. Use the angled cake spatula to cover the cake completely with a very thin layer of icing (this is called the crumb coat) to help reduce the amount of crumbs in the final coat of icing. Set the two-tiered 8-inch (20.5 cm) cake aside.

3. Repeat this process with the 6-inch (15 cm) cake layers. Once the same process has been completed on the 6-inch (15 cm) cake layers, allow them to dry for 1 hour, or until the icing crusts.

4. Create supports for the smaller cake to sit atop the larger cake by placing the dowels into the top of the 8-inch (20.5 cm) cake. Insert the first dowel down into the cake and use a pen to mark the dowel at the point where it just comes to the top of the cake. Remove the dowel and cut it at that mark. Cut three to four additional dowels or straws to the same length and place them in a circle, approximately 2 inches (5 cm) from the center of the cake, and evenly spaced. Using a large, flat spatula, carefully center and place the 6-inch (15 cm) cake on top of the 8-inch (20.5 cm) cake.

5. Place the cake on a rotating cake turntable. Fill the pastry bag with buttercream frosting. Using Wilton decorating tip #103, start at the bottom tier, and with the widest side of the tip closest to the cake, begin to squeeze pastry bag with even pressure while slowly spinning the cake to create ruffles. Continue decorating the cake until finished with the sides of the 8-inch (20.5 cm) base cake.

6. Once the sides of the 8-inch (20.5 cm) base cake are done, start with the outer edge of the top of the 8-inch (20.5 cm) cake. Holding the decorating tip with the widest end closest to the cake top, use the same technique, spinning the table and squeezing the pastry bag with even pressure to create ruffles around the top of the cake until you meet up with the 6-inch (15 cm) top tier.

7. Use the same technique to decorate the 6-inch (15 cm) top tier until the entire cake top is full of ruffles.

PRINCESS CAKE TOPPER

Cut or rip small strips of fabric scraps to match your table decorations. Tie each strip along a bunting string or baker's twine. Attach string to two lollipop sticks that are wrapped in pink ribbon. Place in the center of your finished cake.

Enchanted Rose Cupcakes

THESE ADORABLE ENCHANTED ROSE CUPCAKES WITH PINK BUTTERCREAM FROSTING WILL CATCH EVERYONE'S ATTENTION, ESPECIALLY WHEN DISPLAYED ON AN EQUALLY CHARMING CAKE PLATE SURROUNDED BY FRESH PINK ROSES OR CUT FLOWERS. THE GORGEOUS PINK ROSES ARE EASY TO MAKE WITH A PASTRY BAG AND TIP AND A LITTLE PRACTICE. THE ROSES DON'T NEED TO BE ABSOLUTELY PERFECT, AS EACH ROSE IS UNIQUE.

MAKES 48 MINI CUPCAKES

INGREDIENTS

1 (18.25-OUNCE [517 G]) BOX DUNCAN HINES FRENCH VANILLA CAKE MIX

1 (3.4-OUNCE [110 G)]) BOX JELL-O FRENCH VANILLA INSTANT PUDDING AND PIE FILLING, DRY

1 CUP (235 ML) WATER

⅓ CUP (80 ML) OIL

4 EGGS

1 BATCH BUTTERCREAM FROSTING (PAGE 10)

AMERICOLOR PALE PINK SOFT GEL PASTE COLOR

YOU WILL NEED

2 MINI CUPCAKE TRAYS

48 MINI PAPER CUPCAKE LINERS

COOKIE SCOOP

1 LARGE PASTRY BAG

#1M WILTON DECORATING TIP

DIRECTIONS

1. Preheat the oven to 350°F (180°C). Line the mini cupcake trays with 48 mini paper cupcake liners. Set the prepared trays aside.

2. In a large bowl, and using an electric stand mixer fitted with a paddle attachment, beat the cake mix, pudding mix, water, oil and eggs on medium speed for 2 to 3 minutes, or until well blended. Scrape down the sides of the bowl, and mix again until all the ingredients are incorporated.

3. Using a cookie scoop, place one small scoop of cake batter into each paper liner (filling about three-quarters full), dividing evenly between the cupcake trays to create a perfectly even batch of cupcakes.

4. Bake the cupcakes for 10–13 minutes, or until a toothpick inserted into the center comes out clean. Remove the cupcakes from the oven and place the trays on wire cooling racks for 5 minutes.

5. Take the cupcakes out of the trays and allow them to cool completely on the wire racks before decorating.

6. Meanwhile, make the buttercream frosting. Add pink food coloring to the frosting until it reaches the desired shade.

7. Trim tip of pastry bag. Drop Wilton tip #1M into bag and fill with frosting.

8. Starting from the center of the cupcake top, begin to squeeze decorating bag, using consistent pressure, and in a clockwise motion, swirl around to create a rose.

Charming Chocolate Cupcake Truffles

THE BEST PART OF THIS MINIATURE DESSERT IS THAT IT CAN WORK FOR ANY CAKE POP RECIPE AND THE CANDY COATING CAN BE CHANGED TO ANY COLOR WITH A FEW DROPS OF CANDY OIL. GUESTS ARE ALWAYS SURPRISED WHEN THEY DISCOVER THEY CAN EAT THE ENTIRE TRUFFLE. THE CUPCAKE LINER IS ACTUALLY EDIBLE!

MAKES 40 TO 45 CUPCAKE BITES

INGREDIENTS

COOKING SPRAY AND FLOUR, FOR PAN

1 (18.25-OUNCE [517 G]) BOX DUNCAN HINES DEVIL'S FOOD CAKE MIX

1 (3.4-OUNCE [110 G]) BOX JELL-O CHOCOLATE INSTANT PUDDING AND PIE FILLING, DRY

1 CUP (235 ML) WATER

⅓ CUP (80 ML) OIL

4 LARGE EGGS

½ TO ¾ CUP (120 ML TO 175 ML) CHOCOLATE BUTTERCREAM FROSTING (PAGE 10)

6 CUPS (1.4 KG) VANILLA CANDY MELTS

PINK CANDY OIL

40 TO 45 PINK SIXLET CANDIES

YOU WILL NEED

9 × 13-INCH (23 × 33 CM) BAKING PAN OR CASSEROLE DISH

DISPOSABLE PASTRY BAG

PEANUT BUTTER CUP CHOCOLATE MOLDS

DIRECTIONS

1. Preheat the oven to 350°F (180°C). Coat the 9 × 13-inch (23 × 33 cm) baking pan with cooking spray or grease and flour the pan, tapping out the excess flour. Set aside.

2. In a large bowl, and using an electric stand mixer fitted with a paddle attachment, beat the cake mix, pudding mix, water, oil and eggs on medium speed for 2 to 3 minutes, or until well blended.

3. Pour the batter into the prepared cake pan. Place the pan in the preheated oven, and bake for 35 to 40 minutes, or until a toothpick inserted into the center comes out clean.

4. Remove the pan from the oven and place on a wire cooling rack for 25 to 30 minutes. Let cool completely before making the cake pops.

5. Mash up the cake and place in a large bowl. Using an electric stand mixer fitted with a paddle attachment, mix the cake and ½ to ¾ cup (120 to 175 ml) of chocolate buttercream frosting on medium speed until well blended and the mixture can be molded into a ball.

6. Measure and roll the mixture into 1 tablespoon-size balls, place on a cookie sheet and refrigerate for 1 hour, or until firm.

7. Melt the candy melts in a microwave-safe bowl in 30-second increments at 40% power for about 1½ minutes, stirring as needed until smooth. Remove the bowl from the microwave. Add enough pink candy oil to create the desired bright pink color. Fill a disposable pastry bag with the melted candy. Trim tip of pastry bag and squirt melted candy into the bottom of the peanut butter cup molds, about one-third full.

8. Remove the cake balls from the refrigerator and place each one inside a candy-coated mold. This will make your bright pink melted candy fill the mold. It will look like a naked cupcake. Once all the mold cavities are filled, refrigerate for an additional 10 minutes or so.

9. Add the leftover white candy melts to the melted pink candy to create a lighter pink color. Remove the molds from the refrigerator, and dip the tops of each Chocolate Truffle into the lighter pink melted candy. Top each cupcake with one pink Sixlet candy. Set aside to dry before serving.

Sparkle Rice Krispie Wands

EVERY FAIRY GODMOTHER NEEDS A MAGIC WAND, AND THESE SIMPLE WANDS DO JUST THE TRICK. THEY CAN'T GET MUCH EASIER THAN PINK RICE KRISPIE TREATS ON A LOLLIPOP STICK, DIPPED IN PINK SANDING SUGAR. ATTACH A FEW PINK RIBBONS AND BEFORE YOU KNOW IT, ALL THE LITTLE PRINCESSES WILL BE LIVING DELICIOUSLY EVER AFTER.

Makes 12 to 15 wands

INGREDIENTS

COOKING SPRAY

3 TABLESPOONS (42 G) BUTTER OR MARGARINE

1 (10-OUNCE [280 G]) PACKAGE MINI MARSHMALLOWS (4 CUPS)

PINK FOOD COLORING

6 CUPS (150 G) RICE KRISPIES CEREAL

PALE PINK SANDING SUGAR

YOU WILL NEED

9 × 13-INCH (23 × 33 CM) BAKING PAN OR CASSEROLE DISH

STAR COOKIE CUTTER

12 TO 15 LOLLIPOP STICKS

PINK RIBBON

STYROFOAM

ROSE PETALS (I USE REAL, UNSPRAYED PETALS BUT ARTIFICIAL ARE OK)

DIRECTIONS

1. Lightly oil or spray a 9 × 13-inch (23 × 33 cm) baking pan with cooking spray.

2. Line the bottom of a pretty vintage bowl or tray with a piece of Styrofoam. Set aside.

3. In a large saucepan over low heat and melt the butter. Add the marshmallows and stir until melted and smooth. Remove the pan from the heat. Add the pink food coloring and stir again.

4. Add the Rice Krispies and stir until completely coated. Pat into the prepared baking pan and let cool completely.

5. Once set, cut out star shapes, using the star cookie cutter.

6. Insert one lollipop stick into the bottom of each star.

7. Dip the stars in a bowl filled with pink sanding sugar.

8. Attach pink ribbons to the striped straws to create your "wands."

9. Insert the Rice Krispie Wands into the Styrofoam and arrange the rose petals to cover.

Marshmallow Pillow Pops

ANOTHER EASY DESSERT, THESE DAINTY MARSHMALLOW PILLOW POPS ARE MELT-IN-YOUR-MOUTH TREATS. A PRETTY BOW TIED TO THE END OF THE STICK IS A PERFECT TOUCH FOR THESE LIGHT-AS-CLOUD GOODIES.

MAKES 24 MARSHMALLOW POPS

INGREDIENTS

1 PACKAGE LARGE MARSHMALLOWS (YOU WON'T USE THE ENTIRE PACKAGE, BUT THIS WILL PROVIDE OPTIONS WHEN LOOKING FOR PERFECTLY SHAPED MARSHMALLOWS IN THE BAG.)

1 (12-OUNCE [340 G]) PACKAGE PINK CANDY MELTS

PINK SANDING SUGAR

YOU WILL NEED

24 (5-INCH [12.5 CM]) LOLLIPOP STICKS

PIECE OF STYROFOAM

PINK BAKER'S TWINE, OR PINK RIBBON (OPTIONAL)

DIRECTIONS

1. Place the sanding sugar in a small bowl and set aside. Select two dozen marshmallows from the package and insert a lollipop stick into the bottom of each. Set aside. Keep the Styrofoam close at hand so you can quickly and easily insert the finished marshmallow pops in it.

2. Melt the candy melts in a microwave-safe bowl in 30-second increments at 40% power for about 1½ minutes, stirring as needed until smooth. Remove the bowl from the microwave.

3. Dip each marshmallow stick into the melted candy so that about half of the marshmallow is submerged. Remove the marshmallow from the melted candy and use a spoon to sprinkle the pink sanding sugar over the pink chocolate until it is completely covered. Place the finished marshmallow pops upside down on a sheet of Styrofoam to dry for at least 5 minutes before serving.

4. If you wish, tie a piece of baker's twine into a bow around the lollipop stick for decoration.

Bibbidi Bobbidi Blue Cake Pops

EVERYONE ADORES CAKE POPS, AND THESE MOUTHWATERING TREATS ARE THE PERFECT SIZE FOR SNACKING. TO COORDINATE WITH THE PRINCESS TEA PARTY THEME, BLUE CANDY-COATED CAKE BALLS ARE SANDED WITH SPARKLY BLUE SUGAR TO TEMPT ALL THE PRINCESSES—AND PRINCES—INTO GOING BACK FOR MORE.

MAKES 40 CAKE POPS

INGREDIENTS

BLUE SANDING SUGAR

COOKING SPRAY OR CRISCO OR BUTTER PLUS FLOUR, FOR PAN

1 (18.25-OUNCE [517 G]) BOX DUNCAN HINES FRENCH VANILLA CAKE MIX

1 (3.4-OUNCE [110 G]) BOX JELL-O FRENCH VANILLA INSTANT PUDDING AND PIE FILLING, DRY

1 CUP (235 ML) WATER

⅓ CUP (80 ML) OIL

4 LARGE EGGS

½ TO ¾ CUP (120 TO 175 ML) BUTTERCREAM FROSTING (PAGE 10)

WHITE CANDY MELTS

BLUE CANDY OIL

BLUE SANDING SUGAR

YOU WILL NEED

9 × 13-INCH (23 × 33 CM) BAKING PAN OR CASSEROLE DISH

40 LOLLIPOP STICKS

STYROFOAM

PINK RIBBON FOR BOWS

DIRECTIONS

1. Place the blue sanding sugar in a shallow bowl and set aside.

2. Preheat the oven to 350°F (180°C). Coat the 9 × 13-inch (23 × 33 cm) baking pan with cooking spray or grease and flour the pan, tapping out the excess flour. Set aside.

3. In a large bowl, and using an electric stand mixer fitted with a paddle attachment, beat the cake mix, pudding mix, water, oil and eggs on medium speed for 2 to 3 minutes, or until well blended. Pour the batter into the prepared cake pan. Place the pan in the preheated oven, and bake for 35 to 40 minutes, or until a toothpick inserted into the center comes out clean.

4. Remove the pan from the oven and place on a wire cooling rack for 25 to 30 minutes. Let cool completely before making the cake pops.

5. Mash up the cake and place in a large bowl. Using an electric stand mixer fitted with a paddle attachment, mix the cake and ½ to ¾ cup (120 to 175 ml) of frosting on medium speed until well blended and the mixture can be molded into a ball.

6. Measure and roll the mixture into 1 tablespoon-size balls and place on a cookie sheet. Refrigerate for 1 hour, or until firm.

7. Melt the candy melts in a microwave-safe bowl in 30-second increments at 40% power for about 1½ minutes, stirring as needed until smooth. Remove the bowl from the microwave. Add the blue candy oil to create a light blue color.

8. Remove the pops from the refrigerator. Dip each lollipop stick ¼ inch (6 mm) into the melted candy. Insert the sticks into all the cake balls.

9. Proceed to dip each entire cake ball down into the melted candy. Use a spoon to sprinkle the blue sanding sugar over the cake pops until completely covered. Stand the pops up in a sheet of Styrofoam to dry for at least 5 minutes.

10. Tie a piece of baker's twine or narrow blue ribbon tied into a bow at the end of the stick for decoration.

Princess Tea Party Jenny Cookies

THESE DELIGHTFUL JENNY COOKIES ARE SURE TO WOW ALL YOUR PRINCESSES AND THEIR PARENTS. IF YOU WISH TO MAKE ALL FIVE SUGAR COOKIES ON THE PRINCESS TEA PARTY DESSERT TABLE AS THEY'RE PICTURED, MAKE ONE BATCH OF BUTTERCREAM FROSTING AS DIRECTED ON PAGE 10, DIVIDE AND TINT EACH WITH THE APPROPRIATE COLORS. ATTACH WILTON DECORATING TIPS AND COUPLERS TO EACH OF THE PASTRY BAGS AND FILL WITH EQUAL AMOUNTS OF FROSTING; ONE WITH WHITE FROSTING, LIGHT PINK, DARK PINK, AND LIGHT BLUE. IT SOUNDS LIKE A LOT OF WORK, BUT IN REALITY, IT ISN'T. YOU'LL BE MAKING JUST ONE BATCH OF SUGAR COOKIE DOUGH AND USING IT FOR ALL FIVE COOKIE SHAPES. THE SAME GOES FOR DECORATING THE COOKIES, AS THEY ALL USE THE SAME FROSTING. SEE PAGE 12 FOR THE COOKIE INGREDIENTS AND DIRECTIONS. BEFORE BAKING THE HEART-SHAPED COOKIES, USE A SHARP KNIFE TO CUT OUT A NOTCH FOR THE COOKIE TO HANG OFF OF THE SIDE OF A TEACUP.

MAKES ABOUT 24 COOKIES

YOU WILL NEED

ROLLING PIN

2 NONSTICK COOKIE SHEETS

COOKIE SPATULA

TIARA (CROWN) COOKIE CUTTER

CARRIAGE COOKIE CUTTER

GLASS SLIPPER COOKIE CUTTER

MAGIC WAND COOKIE CUTTER

HEART COOKIE CUTTER

4 PASTRY BAGS

SHARP KNIFE

4 #4 WILTON DECORATING TIPS

4 WILTON COUPLERS

AMERICOLOR SOFT GEL PASTE COLORS TO MAKE LIGHT PINK, DARK PINK AND LIGHT BLUE FROSTING

PINK SANDING SUGAR

Magic Wand Sugar Cookies

INGREDIENTS

DARK PINK BUTTERCREAM

BLUE BUTTERCREAM

PINK SANDING SUGAR

To decorate the magic wand cookies, place dark pink and blue buttercream frosting in separate pastry bags each fitted with a #4 Wilton decorating tip. Place some pink sanding sugar on a plate and set aside. Begin by outlining and filling the star with pink frosting. Turn the cookie upside down and set it in the sugar until the top of the cookie is coated and adheres to the frosting. Turn the cookie right side up and ice the wand with blue frosting.

(continued)

Royal Carriage Cookies

INGREDIENTS
BLUE BUTTERCREAM
DARK PINK BUTTERCREAM
LIGHT PINK BUTTERCREAM
WHITE BUTTERCREAM
BLUE SANDING SUGAR

To decorate the carriage cookies, place light blue, light pink and white (uncolored) buttercream frosting into separate pastry bags each fitted with a #4 Wilton decorating tip. Begin by outlining the carriage with blue frosting, stopping the outline at the top of the carriage's wheels, so that part of the cookie is left unfrosted. Use white frosting to outline the wheels. Once outlined, draw approximately four small lines from the center of the wheel out toward the edge to create spokes. Outline the carriage's windows with white frosting. I like to outline them in the shape of curtains (as shown in the image on page 45), but you can also outline the windows in the shape of a square. Use blue frosting to fill in the outline of the carriage with horizontal lines from one edge of the carriage to the other. Be sure to keep blue frosting outside of the white window and wheel borders. Use pink frosting to fill in the carriage's windows, running it horizontally from one edge of the white border to the other. Place a dot of light pink frosting in the center of each carriage wheel, where the spokes meet. If you like, use white frosting to add a bit of detail to the carriage as shown in the image. To do this, make three small dots evenly spaced over the top of the carriage windows and a swirl in the area just over the carriage's front tire.

Tea Party Heart Cookies
(HEART COOKIES WITH CORNER CUT OUT)

INGREDIENTS
PINK BUTTERCREAM

To decorate the teacup heart cookies, place dark pink buttercream frosting in a pastry bag fitted with a #4 Wilton decorating tip. Begin by outlining the entire heart with pink frosting. Starting at the top of the heart, ice the cookie with a back-and-forth motion until the outline is filled in.

Princess Tiara Cookies

INGREDIENTS
LIGHT PINK BUTTERCREAM
DARK PINK BUTTERCREAM
PINK SANDING SUGAR

To decorate the princess tiara cookies, place light pink and dark pink buttercream frosting into separate pastry bags, each fitted with a #4 Wilton decorating tip. Begin by drawing round baubles on the top of the crown with dark pink buttercream. Turn cookie upside down in a plate of pink sanding sugar so the sugar adheres to the frosting. Turn the cookie right side up. Using pale pink icing bag, outline crown shape. Finish by filling in the frosting outline with horizontal lines until entire crown is filled.

Glass Slipper Sugar Cookies

INGREDIENTS
BLUE BUTTERCREAM
LIGHT PINK BUTTERCREAM

To decorate the glass slipper cookies, place light pink and light blue buttercream frosting in separate pastry bags each fitted with a #4 Wilton decorating tip. Begin by outlining the shoe with blue frosting. To make the shoe look like a delicate glass slipper, make the shoe outline narrow, leaving some undecorated cookie outside of the outline as shown in the image on page 45. Fill in the outline with blue frosting, running it horizontally from one edge of the outline to the other, until the entire shoe is filled in. Use pink buttercream to decorate the top of the shoe just above the toe with a heart or circle shape, approximately 1 centimeter in diameter.

3

Love Is Sweet

MY HUSBAND AND I WERE MARRIED ON VALENTINE'S DAY. WE HADN'T PLANNED ON IT, BUT THE WEDDING VENUE WE CHOSE HAPPENED TO HAVE A CANCELLATION ON FEBRUARY 14, 2004, SO WE TOOK IT. I'M NOT AN ULTRA-ROMANTIC, GET-MARRIED-ON-VALENTINE'S DAY KIND OF GIRL, BUT I RAN WITH THE THEME.

YOU COULD SAY THIS WAS MY FIRST BIG PARTY. I SPENT MONTHS PLANNING, CRAFTING AND CREATING. I SCOURED THRIFT STORES AND ANTIQUE SHOPS FOR VINTAGE MASON JARS (TEN YEARS AGO THEY WEREN'T THE OVERDONE DECOR THAT THEY ARE TODAY—IN FACT, MY BRIDESMAIDS THOUGHT I WAS INSANE WHEN I ASKED IF THEY HAD ANY OLD JARS I COULD USE FOR MY TABLE CENTERPIECES). WHEN I FINALLY GATHERED ENOUGH, I FILLED THEM WITH FLOWERS AND VOTIVE CANDLES, TIED EACH WITH COORDINATING RED RIBBON AND GROUPED THEM IN THE CENTER OF EACH RECEPTION TABLE. I CREATED HANGING HEART GARLANDS MADE FROM HEART-SHAPED DOILIES, CRAFTED WEDDING PROGRAMS TO LOOK LIKE LITTLE VALENTINE ENVELOPES AND MADE SURE ALL THINGS RED AND HEART-SHAPED WERE ADDED TO EVERY CORNER OF THE VENUE. MY HUSBAND SURPRISED ME WITH FIREWORKS THAT WENT OFF IN FRONT OF THE GIGANTIC WINDOW WHERE WE EXCHANGED "I DOS" AND KISSED. IN THAT MOMENT, I REALLY WAS DREAMY AND ROMANTIC.

My inspiration for creating the Sweetheart dessert table starts with my favorite colors, cake plates and desserts. Like a wedding, the sweetheart table should be filled with all the things you love. And if I were to do my wedding all over again (because, just admit it, we all want to) I'd choose a blush pink, my favorite jadeite and pink milk glass cake plates, and fill the table with my favorite desserts.

SETTING THE TABLE

Try to use a vintage white sideboard table as the canvas for your table. I love its narrow depth and height, compared with a standard-size table.

In keeping the love theme, use chocolate-dipped Rice Krispie treats in the shape of hearts, heart-shaped sugar cookies and top a cake with sparkly gold wooden heart toppers. I love the fluffy, white wedding dress cookies on my favorite Jeannette shell pink cake plates and sweet ruffled pink cupcakes on jadeite. To add a pop of pink to the table, make a batch of strawberry sandwich cookies, sprinkled with powdered sugar. Dust the cake pops with edible gold glitter to coordinate with the sparkly gold heart cake topper.

My mint-colored cake plates came from my extensive jadeite collection in addition to vintage pink milk cake stands. I know not everyone owns gobs of jadeite like me, though. You can find them on eBay, Etsy or even rent from a local party shop.

LOVE IS SWEET DESSERTS

- ♥ **Hearts of Gold Rustic Cake**
- ♥ **Pink Vintage Ruffle Cupcakes**
- ♥ **Filled with Love Cake Pops**
- ♥ **Sweet as Can Be Rice Krispie Treats**
- ♥ **Whipped Vanilla Cream Cupcakes**
- ♥ **Peanut Butter Bliss Cookies**
- ♥ **Strawberry Sweetheart Cookies**
- ♥ **Heart Cookies**
- ♥ **Wedding Dress Cookies**

Hearts of Gold Rustic Cake

PLACE THIS CAKE IN THE CENTER OF THE TABLE AS A FOCAL POINT. THE GLITTERED HEART TOPPERS ARE MADE BY MERELY HOT GLUING WOODEN HEARTS TO WOOD DOWELS AND PAINTING WITH GOLD GLITTER SPRAY (EASILY SOURCED AT VARIOUS CRAFT STORES).

Note: This cake is large and uses five boxes of cake mix. The bowl of a standard electric stand mixer is not large enough to hold ingredients for such a large amount. You may have to mix the batter and bake the cake in two or three batches.

MAKES ONE 7-INCH (18 CM) AND 9-INCH (23 CM) TIERED CAKE

CAKE INGREDIENTS

COOKING SPRAY OR CRISCO OR BUTTER PLUS FLOUR, FOR PANS

5 (18.25-OUNCE [517 G]) BOXES DUNCAN HINES WHITE CAKE MIX

5 (3.4-OUNCE [110 G]) BOXES JELL-O VANILLA INSTANT PUDDING AND PIE FILLING, DRY

5 CUPS (1.18 L) WATER

1⅔ CUPS (400 ML) VEGETABLE OIL

20 LARGE EGG WHITES

3 BATCHES BUTTERCREAM FROSTING (PAGE 10)

YOU WILL NEED

4 (9 × 2-INCH [23 × 5 CM] AND 2 (7 × 2-INCH [18 × 5 CM]) ROUND NONSTICK CAKE PANS

CAKE CUTTER OR LONG, SERRATED KNIFE

2 ROUND CARDBOARD OR PLASTIC CAKE BOARDS

OFFSET ANGLED SPATULA

6 (¼-INCH [6 MM]-THICK) DOWELS OR THICK PLASTIC STRAWS

LARGE, FLAT SPATULA

CAKE DECORATING TURNTABLE

LARGE DECORATING SPATULA

DIRECTIONS

1. Preheat the oven to 350°F (180°C). Coat both the 7-inch (18 cm) and 9-inch (23 cm) round cake pans with cooking spray, or grease and flour the pans, tapping out the excess flour. Set the prepared pans aside.

2. In a large bowl, and using an electric stand mixer fitted with a paddle attachment, beat the cake mix, pudding mix, water, oil and eggs on medium speed for 2 to 3 minutes, or until well blended. Scrape the sides of the bowl and mix again until all the ingredients are incorporated.

3. Pour the batter into the prepared cake pans, filling each one approximately three-quarters full.

4. Place the pans in the preheated oven, on the middle rack. Bake the 7-inch (18 cm) and 9-inch (23 cm) cakes for 30 to 35 minutes, or until a toothpick inserted into the center comes out clean. Depending on the size of your oven you may have to bake the cakes in two or three batches.

5. Remove the pans from the oven and place on wire cooling racks for 25 to 30 minutes. Run a knife around the edges of the cakes, flip the pans over and gently extract the cakes. Return the cakes to the wire racks and finish cooling completely before frosting and decorating. After the layers are cooled, freeze or refrigerate the cakes for 1 hour before decorating to reduce crumbs to make for a smoother icing process.

6. Meanwhile, make the three batches of buttercream frosting.

TO ASSEMBLE AND DECORATE THE CAKE

1. Before decorating, trim the crowns from the cake tops with a cake cutter or long, serrated knife so they are flat and even.

2. Place one of the 9-inch (23 cm) cakes on a cake board cut side up. Using the angled cake spatula, spread about ½ cup (120 ml) of buttercream frosting evenly across the top of the cake layer. Place the second, third and fourth 9-inch (23 cm) cakes on top of the first, with the cut sides on the bottom, and spreading the buttercream frosting between each. Use the angled cake spatula to cover the cake completely with a very thin layer of icing (or crumb coat) to help reduce the amount of crumbs in the final coat of icing. Set the four-tiered 9-inch (23 cm) cake aside.

3. Repeat this process with the 7-inch (18 cm) cake layers, using another ½ cup (120 ml) of buttercream frosting between the layers, and icing the sides and top of the cake. Once the same process has been completed on the 7-inch (18 cm) cake layers, allow them to dry for 1 hour, or until the icing crusts.

4. Create supports for the smaller cake to sit atop the larger cake by placing the dowels into the top of the 9-inch (23 cm) cake. Insert the first dowel into the cake and use a pen to mark the dowel at the point where it just comes to the top of the cake. Remove the dowel and cut it at that mark. Cut four to five additional dowels or straws to the same length and place them in a circle, approximately 2 inches (5 cm) from the center of the cake, and evenly spaced. Using a large, flat spatula, carefully center and place the 7-inch (18 cm) cake on top of the 9-inch (23 cm) cake.

5. Place the cake on a rotating cake turntable. Starting at the top of the cake, and using a large decorating spatula, frost the top of the cake. Continue with the sides of both tiers, icing it with a rough spackled finish, as shown in the photos.

Pink Vintage Ruffle Cupcakes

THE RUFFLE TECHNIQUE IS MY ABSOLUTE FAVORITE WAY TO DECORATE A CUPCAKE.
IT'S FEMININE AND SWEET, PERFECT FOR WEDDINGS, SHOWERS AND BIRTHDAY PARTIES.
CAN YOU IMAGINE HOW BEAUTIFUL IT WOULD BE FOR A BALLERINA-THEMED PARTY?

MAKES 24 CUPCAKES

INGREDIENTS

1 (18.25-OUNCE [517 G]) BOX DUNCAN HINES COCONUT SUPREME CAKE MIX

1 (3.4-OUNCE [110 G]) BOX JELL-O COCONUT CREAM INSTANT PUDDING AND PIE FILLING, DRY

1 CUP (235 ML) WATER

⅓ CUP (80 ML) OIL

4 LARGE EGGS

1 BATCH BUTTERCREAM FROSTING (PAGE 10)

AMERICOLOR PALE PINK SOFT GEL PASTE COLOR

YOU WILL NEED

2 STANDARD-SIZE CUPCAKE TRAYS

24 STANDARD PAPER CUPCAKE LINERS

SMALL COOKIE SCOOP

CAKE DECORATING TURNTABLE

1 LARGE PASTRY BAG

#104 WILTON DECORATING TIP

WILTON COUPLER

DIRECTIONS

1. Preheat the oven to 350°F (180°C). Line the cupcake trays with paper cupcake liners. Set the prepared pans aside.

2. In a large bowl, and using an electric stand mixer fitted with a paddle attachment, beat the cake mix, pudding mix, water, oil and eggs on medium speed for 2 to 3 minutes, or until well blended. Scrape down the sides of the bowl, and mix again until all the ingredients are incorporated.

3. Using a cookie scoop, fill each paper liner with batter to fill the liner about two-thirds full, dividing evenly between the cupcake trays.

4. Bake the cupcakes for 18 to 20 minutes, or until a toothpick inserted into the center comes out clean, or tops spring back when lightly touched. Remove the cupcakes from the oven and place the trays on wire cooling racks for 5 minutes. Take the cupcakes out of the trays and allow them to cool completely on the wire racks before decorating.

5. Meanwhile, make the one batch of buttercream frosting. Add pink food coloring to the frosting until it reaches the desired shade. Attach Wilton decorating tip #104 and the coupler to the pastry bag and fill with frosting.

6. To decorate, place a cupcake on the cake decorating turntable. Holding the pastry bag at a 45-degree angle, and with the fat end of the decorating tip facing down closest to the cupcake, begin squeezing the icing at the outer edge of the cupcake while spinning the cake turntable, to create a ruffled look. Continue spinning and squeezing the icing around toward the center of the cupcake while creating overlapping ruffles until the entire cupcake is filled.

Filled with Love Cake Pops

THIS DESSERT IS RICH AND CREAMY. ITS RED VELVET FLAVOR, COVERED IN A SMOOTH CANDY COATING, HAS EVERYONE SMITTEN—IT'S ONE OF MY MOST POPULAR DESSERTS.

MAKES 40 CAKE POPS

INGREDIENTS

COOKING SPRAY OR CRISCO OR BUTTER PLUS FLOUR, FOR PAN

1 (18.25 OUNCE [517 G]) BOX DUNCAN HINES RED VELVET CAKE MIX

1 (3.4-OUNCE [110 G]) BOX JELL-O CHOCOLATE INSTANT PUDDING AND PIE FILLING, DRY

1 CUP (235 ML) WATER

⅓ CUP (80 ML) OIL

4 LARGE EGGS

½ TO ¾ CUP (120 TO 175 ML) DUNCAN HINES CREAM CHEESE FROSTING

3 (12-OUNCE [340 G]) PACKAGES WHITE CANDY MELTS

GOLD DISCO DUST

YOU WILL NEED

9 × 13-INCH (23 × 33 CM) BAKING PAN OR CASSEROLE DISH

40 (5-INCH [12.5 CM]) LOLLIPOP STICKS

SMALL PAINT- OR CRAFT BRUSH

STYROFOAM

PINK RIBBON

DIRECTIONS

1. Preheat the oven to 350°F (180°C). Coat the 9 × 13-inch (23 × 33 cm) baking pan with cooking spray or grease and flour the pan, tapping out excess the flour. Set aside.

2. In a large bowl, and using an electric stand mixer fitted with a paddle attachment, beat the cake mix, pudding mix, water, oil and eggs on medium speed for 2 to 3 minutes, or until well blended. Scrape the sides of the bowl and mix again until all the ingredients are incorporated.

3. Pour the batter into the prepared baking pan. Place the pan in the preheated oven, and bake for 35 to 40 minutes, or until a toothpick inserted into the center comes out clean.

4. Remove the pan from the oven and place on a wire cooling rack for 25 to 30 minutes. Let cool completely before making the cake pops.

5. Mash up the cake and place in a large bowl. Using an electric stand mixer fitted with a paddle attachment, mix the cake and ½ to ¾ cup (120 to 175 ml) of the frosting on medium speed until moist and well blended and the mixture can be molded into a ball.

6. Measure and roll the mixture into tablespoon-size balls and place on a cookie sheet. Refrigerate for 1 hour, or until firm.

7. Melt the candy melts in separate microwave-safe bowls in 30-second increments at 40% power for about 2 to 3 minutes, stirring as needed until smooth.

8. Remove the pops from the refrigerator. Dip each lollipop stick ¼ inch (6 mm) into the melted candy. Insert the sticks into all the cake balls. (The melted candy will adhere the lollipop sticks to cake balls to prevent them from falling off the sticks when dipping.) Proceed to dip the entire cake balls down into the melted candy.

9. Dip the paintbrush into Disco Dust and gently tap to dust the pops while the coating is still tacky. Stand up the pops in a sheet of Styrofoam to dry.

10. Add a pink ribbon bow to each stick.

Sweet As Can Be Rice Krispie Treats

TO GIVE THESE HEART-SHAPED RICE KRISPIE TREATS A LITTLE EXTRA LOVE, I DIPPED HALF IN MELTED CANDY AND DRIZZLED PINK OVER THE TOP. ADD A FEW DROPS OF FOOD COLORING TO YOUR RICE KRISPIE BATTER FOR DIFFERENT COLORED TREATS.

MAKES 12 TO 15 TREATS

INGREDIENTS

VEGETABLE SPRAY

3 TABLESPOONS (42 G) BUTTER OR MARGARINE

1 (10-OUNCE [280 G]) PACKAGE MINI MARSHMALLOWS (4 CUPS)

6 CUPS (150 G) RICE KRISPIES CEREAL

2 (12-OUNCE [340 G]) PACKAGES WHITE CANDY MELTS

PINK CANDY OIL

YOU WILL NEED

9 × 13-INCH (23 × 33 CM) BAKING PAN OR CASSEROLE DISH

LARGE HEART COOKIE CUTTER

DISPOSABLE PASTRY BAG

STYROFOAM

WAXED PAPER

DIRECTIONS

1. Lightly oil or spray the 9 × 13-inch (23 × 33 cm) baking pan with vegetable spray.

2. In a large saucepan over low heat, melt the butter. Add the marshmallows and stir until melted and smooth. Remove the pan from the heat.

3. Add the Rice Krispies and stir until completely coated. Pat into the prepared baking pan and let cool completely to set.

4. Once set, cut out heart shapes, using the cookie cutter.

5. Melt the candy melts in a microwave-safe bowl in 30-second increments at 40% power for about 1½ to 2 minutes, stirring as needed until smooth.

6. Dip half of each heart in the melted candy and lay flat on waxed paper to dry.

7. Add a few drops of pink candy oil to the melted candy and stir. Place the pink candy in the disposable pastry bag. Cut off the tip with scissors to make a very small hole, and drizzle over the white-dipped heart. Return to the waxed paper and let dry.

Whipped Vanilla Cream Cupcakes

THE BEAUTY OF THESE YUMMY VANILLA CUPCAKES IS THEIR ADAPTABILITY. SIMPLY DIP IN ANY COLORED SPRINKLE, CRYSTAL OR SANDING SUGAR TO COORDINATE WITH YOUR EVENT. THE HEART MOLD CAN BE ANY COLOR YOU WISH WITH JUST A FEW DROPS OF CANDY OIL.

MAKES 48 MINI CUPCAKES

INGREDIENTS

1 (12-OUNCE [340 G]) PACKAGE WHITE CANDY MELTS

1 (18.25-OUNCE [517 G]) BOX DUNCAN HINES FRENCH VANILLA CAKE MIX

1 (3.4-OUNCE [110 G]) JELL-O INSTANT FRENCH VANILLA PUDDING AND PIE FILLING, DRY

1 CUP (235 ML) WATER

⅓ CUP (80 ML) OIL

4 LARGE EGGS

1 BATCH BUTTERCREAM FROSTING (PAGE 10)

PINK CANDY OIL

GOLD SPRINKLES

YOU WILL NEED

PLASTIC CANDY MOLD FOR HEART DECORATIONS

2 MINI CUPCAKE TRAYS

48 MINI PAPER CUPCAKE LINERS

SMALL COOKIE SCOOP

LARGE PASTRY BAG

#2A WILTON DECORATING TIP OR #804 ATECO TIP

DISPOSABLE PASTRY BAG

DIRECTIONS

1. Melt the candy melts in a microwave-safe bowl in 30-second increments at 40% power for about 1½ minutes, stirring as needed until smooth. Add pink candy oil and stir again. Pour melted candy into disposable pastry bag and trim tip with scissors. Fill the candy mold with the melted candy and chill until set, about 30 minutes. Remove the candies from the mold and set aside.

2. Preheat the oven to 350°F (180°C). Line mini cupcake trays with 48 mini paper cupcake liners. Set the prepared trays aside.

3. In a large bowl, and using an electric stand mixer fitted with a paddle attachment, beat the cake mix, pudding mix, water, oil and eggs on medium speed for 2 to 3 minutes, or until well blended. Scrape the sides of the bowl and mix again until all the ingredients are incorporated.

4. Using a cookie scoop, fill each paper liner with batter to fill the liner about three-quarters full, dividing evenly between the cupcake trays.

5. Bake the cupcakes for 10-13 minutes, or until a toothpick inserted into the center comes out clean, or the tops spring back when lightly touched. Remove the cupcakes from the oven and place the trays on wire cooling racks for 5 minutes. Take the cupcakes out of the trays and allow them to cool completely on wire racks before decorating.

6. Meanwhile, make the buttercream frosting.

7. Fill a bowl with gold sprinkles.

8. Place the #2A Wilton decorating tip inside the pastry bag (no need to use a coupler) and fill with frosting. Pipe the frosting onto the cupcakes and dip the tops upside down in gold sprinkles. Place a pink candy heart on each cupcake.

Peanut Butter Bliss Cookies

POSSIBLY THE MOST BRILLIANT COMBINATION OF INGREDIENTS EVER. THESE ARE MY GO-TO DESSERT WHEN I NEED A LATE-NIGHT SNACK—SIMPLE TO MAKE AND OH SO DELICIOUS TO EAT. CHANGE IT UP BY DIPPING YOUR PEANUT BUTTER FILLED CRACKERS IN MELTED MILK CHOCOLATE.

MAKES 17 COOKIES

INGREDIENTS

3 (12-OUNCE [340 G]) PACKAGES WHITE CANDY MELTS

PINK CANDY OIL

1 PACKAGE (SLEEVE OF 34) RITZ CRACKERS

1 CUP (260 G) SMOOTH PEANUT BUTTER (I LIKE JIF)

1 TABLESPOON GOLD DISCO DUST

YOU WILL NEED

PLASTIC CANDY MOLD FOR SMALL PINK BOW DECORATIONS

2 DISPOSABLE PASTRY BAGS

SMALL PAINT-OR CRAFT BRUSH

WAXED PAPER

DIRECTIONS

1. Melt one package of candy melts in a microwave-safe bowl in 30-second increments at 40% power for about 1½ minutes, stirring as needed until smooth. Add a few drops of pink candy oil to make a bright pink color and stir again. Pour melted candy into disposable pastry bag and trim tip with scissors. Fill the candy mold with the melted candy and chill until set, about 30 minutes. Remove the candies from the mold and set aside.

2. Turn the Ritz crackers upside down on a cookie sheet. Fill a disposable pastry bag with peanut butter. Cut small tip from the pastry bag and pipe a dollop of peanut butter on half of the crackers. Place the remaining crackers on top to make sandwiches.

3. Melt the remaining two bags of candy melts as directed for 1½ to 2 minutes.

4. Using a fork, dip the crackers into the melted candy. Place on waxed paper and let dry.

5. Add a few drops of pink candy oil to the remainder of the melted candy and stir. Dip half of the cookie in the pink candy. Continue until all the cookies are dipped.

6. Dip the paintbrush into Disco Dust and gently tap to dust the cookies while the coating is still tacky. Place the finished treats on waxed paper to dry.

7. Decorate each cookie with a pink candy bow by attaching with a dab of melted candy.

Strawberry Sweetheart Cookies

WHILE THE REST OF THE DESSERT WORLD HAS SWOONED OVER FRENCH MACARONS, I WANT SOMETHING EASIER AND FASTER. THESE MINIATURE STRAWBERRY COOKIES ARE MADE SIMPLE WITH A BOX OF STRAWBERRY CAKE MIX. WITH JUST A COUPLE OF INGREDIENTS, YOU'LL HAVE YOUR OWN VERSION OF A CAKE MIX MACARON. THIS RECIPE IS SIMPLE TO SWITCH WITH OTHER CAKE MIX FLAVORS.

MAKES 18 SANDWICH COOKIES

INGREDIENTS

1 (18.25-OUNCE [517 G]) BOX DUNCAN HINES STRAWBERRY CAKE MIX

⅓ CUP (80 ML) OIL

2 LARGE EGGS

½ BATCH BUTTERCREAM FROSTING (PAGE 10)

CONFECTIONERS' SUGAR FOR DUSTING COOKIES

YOU WILL NEED

2 NONSTICK COOKIE SHEETS

DISPOSABLE PASTRY BAG

SIFTER

DIRECTIONS

1. Preheat the oven to 375°F (190°C).

2. In a large bowl, and using an electric stand mixer fitted with a paddle attachment, beat the cake mix, oil and eggs on medium speed for 2 to 3 minutes, or until well blended. Scrape the sides of the bowl and mix again until all the ingredients are incorporated. The batter will be thick.

3. Using a teaspoon, measure and roll the dough by hand (spraying your hands with nonstick cooking spray—Pam or Crisco—will help), into round balls and place on ungreased cookie sheets.

4. Bake for 7 to 8 minutes, or until the cookies begin to brown around the edges. Let cool on the cookie sheet for 2 minutes before moving to wire racks. Let cool completely.

5. Turn half of the cookies upside down on a cookie sheet. Using a decorating bag with a snipped tip, or a knife, fill half of the cookies with the buttercream frosting. Top with the remaining cookies to make sandwiches.

6. Using the sifter, sprinkle confectioners' sugar over the tops of the cookies. Turn the cookies over and sprinkle the bottoms.

Love Is Sweet Jenny Cookies

I'VE BEEN ASKED MORE TIMES THAN I CAN COUNT FOR ORDERS OF THESE ADORABLE HEART AND WEDDING DRESS COOKIES FOR BRIDES TO GIVE THEIR BRIDESMAIDS. I LOVE THIS IDEA: THE COOKIES ARE SIMPLE TO DECORATE AND MAKE A STUNNING STATEMENT. CHANGE THE COLOR OF THE WEDDING DRESS SASH AND ICING ON THE HEART COOKIE TO COORDINATE YOUR WEDDING COLORS. THESE ALSO MAKE ADORABLE BRIDAL SHOWER FAVORS.

ONE BATCH OF SUGAR COOKIE DOUGH WILL YIELD APPROXIMATELY TWO DOZEN COOKIES, SO YOU'LL HAVE ABOUT A DOZEN OF EACH WEDDING DRESS AND HEART. THESE COOKIES REQUIRE ONLY PALE PINK AND WHITE FROSTING, SO ONE BATCH OF BUTTERCREAM FROSTING WILL BE PLENTY, YOU MAY HAVE EXTRA FROSTING THAT CAN BE STORED FOR LATER USE. ATTACH WILTON DECORATING TIPS AND COUPLERS TO EACH OF THE PASTRY BAGS AND FILL WITH EQUAL AMOUNTS OF FROSTING. SEE PAGES 10-12 IN THE "BASICS" CHAPTER FOR THE COOKIE INGREDIENTS AND DIRECTIONS.

MAKES ABOUT 24 COOKIES

YOU WILL NEED
ROLLING PIN
2 NONSTICK COOKIE SHEETS
COOKIE SPATULA
LARGE HEART COOKIE CUTTER
WEDDING DRESS COOKIE CUTTER
2 DISPOSABLE PASTRY BAGS
1 #4 WILTON DECORATING TIP
2 #18 WILTON DECORATING TIPS
2 WILTON COUPLERS
AMERICOLOR PINK SOFT GEL PASTE
GOLD SPRINKLES

Heart Cookies

INGREDIENTS
PALE PINK BUTTERCREAM

To decorate the heart cookies, use the pastry bag filled with pale pink frosting. Fitted with a #18 Wilton decorating tip, fill in the entire heart with small stars to create a fluffy texture.

Wedding Dress Cookies

INGREDIENTS
WHITE BUTTERCREAM
GOLD SPRINKLES

To decorate the wedding dress cookies, use the pastry bag filled with white frosting. Fitted with a #4 Wilton decorating tip, begin by piping a sash just under the bust of the dress. Turn cookies upside down in a bowl of gold sprinkles making sure they adhere to the frosting sash. Outline the bust of the dress with the #4 decorating tip. Fill in the outline with frosting, running it horizontally until the bust is filled in. Using white frosting and a #18 tip, decorate the bottom of the dress with swirls to completely fill in.

4

Vintage Baby

NOBODY SHARES MY LOVE FOR ALL THINGS VINTAGE LIKE MY AUNT SUSAN. HER HOUSE IS FILLED WITH ANTIQUES, ALWAYS ARRANGED IN CLEVER WAYS YOU'D NEVER IMAGINE. USUALLY, WHEN YOU COMPLIMENT HER, SHE SAYS, "OH, I GOT THAT FOR A DOLLAR!" SHE'S THE ULTIMATE TREASURE SEEKER AND BARGAIN HUNTER. OVER THE YEARS, WE'VE SPENT NUMEROUS AFTERNOONS WALKING THROUGH ANTIQUE STORES TOGETHER, OR SIFTING THROUGH BASEMENTS OF RANDOM ESTATE SALES, EAGER FOR AN INCREDIBLE FIND. WHILE SHE SEARCHES FOR HOME DECOR, I HAVE MY EYE OUT FOR INTERESTING ITEMS FOR MY NEXT PARTY.

When her daughter, my cousin Jill, was pregnant with her first baby, Susan couldn't wait to throw her a baby shower. Obviously, I was in charge of the desserts. We came up with a vintage stork theme. She sewed fabric bunting banners from vintage fabrics, and I strung them behind two old doors, creating an awesome dessert table backdrop. She found a stork piggy bank that we could use as décor, and I used it for my cake topper. We even used an old-fashioned baby scale that we'd found at a garage sale as a cake plate. Never be afraid of picking up funky vintage finds—you never know when they'll come in handy.

We made a great team. Our dessert table overflowed with delicious, easy treats and so can yours. Bake a white cake with raspberry filling and decorate it in a turquoise blue with my swirled buttercream technique (see page 71). Create edible baby rattles from dipped Oreos and paper straws. Decorate sugar cookies in various baby shapes: baby bottles, carriages, rattles and baby bibs. To add dimension to the baby bib cookies, try adding a ribbon tie to each baby bib, attached with melted chocolate. Banana pudding cups served in upcycled glass baby food jars tied with ribbon and a wood spoon are a simple treat. And for a fun party snack, make up a "she's going to 'pop' corn" mix made with kettle corn, dipped pretzels and bite-size Snickers candies drizzled in pink candy melts.

SETTING THE TABLE

My vintage baby dessert table started with a *very* ugly hunter green drop-leaf table I found for free on Craigslist. My husband was skeptical, but all it needed was some baby blue paint and some roughing up with sand paper.

I stood a pair of hinged vintage doors I'd scored from a secondhand store behind my new (old!) blue table and strung three strands of fabric bunting banners from the doors. Since the baby scale was tall, I placed it on the table first and built my table around it. I'd also picked up a wooden box that was colored in the same themed blue and ended up using it to hold the popcorn snack mix perfectly. I used blue, pink, and white cake plates—always aim for variety—and arranged them around the scale and blue popcorn box.

Once my table was set, I filled it in with desserts. The cake made its way to the top of the baby scale, the pudding cups took the stage atop the blue cake plates, individual bagged popcorn mixes sat inside the blue wooden box and I scattered cookies around the table on various plates. A few flower arrangements in antique blue mason jars completed the look. Welcome, baby!

VINTAGE BABY DESSERTS

- ♥ **Swirled Surprise Cake**
- ♥ **Baby Bliss Cupcakes**
- ♥ **Bitty Banana Pudding Cups**
- ♥ **Rattles from Seattle**
- ♥ **Stork Delivery Bites**
- ♥ **She's Going to Pop Corn**
- ♥ **Rattle Cookies**
- ♥ **Baby Buggy Cookies**
- ♥ **Baby Bottle Cookies**
- ♥ **Baby Bib Cookies**

Swirled Surprise Cake

WHITE CAKE ENHANCED WITH A FLAVORFUL RASPBERRY FILLING ISN'T THE ONLY THING HIDING UNDERNEATH THE STUNNING TURQUOISE SWIRLS. BEFORE BAKING YOUR CAKE, TINT YOUR BATTER WITH PINK OR BLUE FOOD COLORING TO REPRESENT THE BABY'S GENDER. SURPRISE GUESTS WITH A "BLUE OR PINK, WHAT DO YOU THINK?" CAKE REVEAL.

Note: This cake is large and uses three boxes of cake mix. The bowl of a standard electric stand mixer is not large enough to hold ingredients for three cakes. You may have to mix the batter and bake the cake in two or more batches.

MAKES ONE 6-INCH (15 CM) AND 8-INCH (20.5 CM) TIERED CAKE

INGREDIENTS

COOKING SPRAY OR CRISCO OR BUTTER PLUS FLOUR, FOR PANS

3 (18.25-OUNCE [517 G]) BOXES DUNCAN HINES WHITE CAKE MIX

3 (3.4-OUNCE [110 G]) BOXES JELL-O INSTANT VANILLA PUDDING AND PIE FILLING, DRY

3 CUPS (700 ML) WATER

1 CUP (240 ML) OIL

12 LARGE EGG WHITES

3 BATCHES BUTTERCREAM FROSTING (PAGE 10)

2 JARS SEEDLESS RASPBERRY JAM OR PRESERVES

AMERICOLOR TURQUOISE SOFT GEL PASTE COLOR

DIRECTIONS

1. Preheat the oven to 350°F (180°C). Coat the 8-inch (20.5 cm) and 6-inch (15 cm) round nonstick cake pans with cooking spray or grease and flour the pans, tapping out excess the flour. Set the prepared pans aside.

2. In a large bowl, and using an electric stand mixer fitted with a paddle attachment, beat the cake mix, pudding mix, water, oil and eggs on medium speed for 2 to 3 minutes, or until well blended. Scrape the sides of the bowl and mix again until all the ingredients are incorporated.

3. Pour batter into the prepared cake pans, filling each one approximately three-quarters full.

4. Place the pans in the preheated oven, on the middle rack. Bake the 6-inch (15 cm) cakes for 25 to 30 minutes, and the 8-inch (20.5 cm) cakes for 30 to 35 minutes, or until a toothpick inserted into the center comes out clean. Depending on the size of the oven, you may need to bake this cake in two batches.

5. Remove the pans from the oven and place on wire cooling racks for 25 to 30 minutes. Run a knife around the edges of the cakes, flip the pans over and gently extract the cakes. Return the cakes to the wire racks and finish cooling completely before frosting and decorating. After the layers are cooled, freeze or refrigerate the cakes for 1 hour before decorating to reduce crumbs and make for a smoother icing process.

6. Meanwhile, make the three batches of buttercream frosting. Add the turquoise food coloring to the frosting until it reaches the desired shade.

(continued)

3 (8 × 2-INCH [20.5 × 5 CM]) AND
2 (6 × 2-INCH [15 × 5 CM]) ROUND
NONSTICK CAKE PANS
CAKE CUTTER OR LONG, SERRATED
KNIFE
2 ROUND CARDBOARD OR PLASTIC
CAKE BOARDS
OFFSET ANGLED SPATULA
LARGE PASTRY BAG
#30 WILTON DECORATING TIP
WILTON COUPLER
6 (¼-INCH [6 MM]-THICK) DOWELS OR
THICK PLASTIC STRAWS
LARGE, FLAT SPATULA
CAKE DECORATING TURNTABLE
LARGE DECORATING SPATULA

TO ASSEMBLE AND DECORATE THE CAKE

7. Before decorating, trim the crowns from the cake tops with a cake cutter or long, serrated knife so they are flat and even.

8. Place one of the 8-inch (20.5 cm) cakes on a cake board cut side up. Using the angled cake spatula, spread about ¾ cup (250 g) of raspberry jam evenly across the top of the cake layer, making sure to stop within an inch (2.5 cm) of the edges. Place the second and third 8-inch (20.5 cm) cakes on top of the first, with the cut sides on the bottom, spreading jam between each layer. Use the angled cake spatula to cover the cake completely with a very thin layer of turquoise frosting (or crumb coat) to help reduce the amount of crumbs in the final coat of icing. Set the three-tiered 8-inch (20.5 cm) cake aside.

9. Repeat this process with the 6-inch (15 cm) cake layers, using another ½ cup (240 g) of raspberry jam between layers, and icing the sides and top of the cake with turquoise frosting. Once the same process has been completed on the 6-inch (15 cm) cake layers, allow them to dry for 1 hour, or until the icing crusts.

10. Attach Wilton decorating tip #30 and coupler to the pastry bag and fill with turquoise frosting. Set aside.

11. Create supports for the smaller cake to sit atop the larger cake by placing the dowels into the top of the 8-inch (20.5 cm) cake. Insert the first dowel into the cake and use a pen to mark the dowel at the point where it just comes to the top of the cake. Remove the dowel and cut it at that mark. Cut four to five additional dowels or straws to the same length and place them in a circle, approximately 2 inches (5 cm) from the center of the cake, and evenly spaced. Make sure the 8-inch (20.5 cm) tier has a smooth icing finish before decorating. Using a large, flat spatula, carefully center and place the 6-inch (15 cm) tier on top of the 8-inch (20.5 cm) cake tier.

12. Place the cake on the rotating cake turntable. Using a large decorating spatula, frost the top of the cake smooth. Using the pastry bag filled with turquoise frosting, and fitted with a #30 decorating tip, hold the bag horizontally, and start from the bottom of the 8-inch (20.5 cm) tier to create rows of swirls. Starting in the middle of the swirl, squeeze the pastry bag and make a few spirals in a counterclockwise motion around the center, ending at the top of the swirl. Don't worry if you end the swirls with a few tails. These will be covered by the next row of swirls. Turn the turntable and make another swirl following the same technique, always ending at the top of the swirl. Continue all the way around the cake until you meet up with the first swirl you created.

13. Continue with the second row of swirls, slightly touching the swirls on the bottom row so there are no gaps or tails showing. Continue each row of swirls in this manner until you reach the top of the 8-inch (20.5 cm) tier.

14. Repeat this technique with the 6-inch (15 cm) tier until both tiers are full of swirls. Starting at the outside edge on the top of the 6-inch (15 cm) tier, create a circle of swirls. Repeat with a second circle of swirls inside the first, and continue until the top of the cake is covered in swirls.

Baby Bliss Cupcakes

HERE, ADORABLE MINIATURE CUPCAKES ARE TOPPED WITH CANDY-COATED BABY BOTTLES.

MAKES 48 MINI CUPCAKES

INGREDIENTS

1 (18.25-OUNCE [517 G]) BOX DUNCAN HINES WHITE CAKE MIX

1 (3.4-OUNCE [110 G]) BOX JELL-O VANILLA INSTANT PUDDING AND PIE FILLING, DRY

1 CUP (235 ML) WATER

⅓ CUP (80 ML) OIL

4 LARGE EGGS

1 BATCH BUTTERCREAM FROSTING (PAGE 10)

1 (12-OUNCE [340 G]) PACKAGE PINK CANDY MELTS

AMERICOLOR TURQUOISE SOFT GEL PASTE COLOR

YOU WILL NEED

PLASTIC CANDY MOLD FOR BABY BOTTLE DECORATIONS

2 MINI CUPCAKE TRAYS

48 MINI PAPER CUPCAKE LINERS

SMALL COOKIE SCOOP

LARGE PASTRY BAG

#1M WILTON DECORATING TIP

DISPOSABLE PASTRY BAG

DIRECTIONS

1. Melt the candy melts in a microwave-safe bowl in 30-second increments at 40% power for about 1½ minutes, stirring as needed until smooth. Pour melted candy into disposable pastry bag and trim tip with scissors. Fill the candy mold with the melted candy and chill until set, about 30 minutes. Remove the candies from the mold and set aside.

2. Preheat the oven to 350°F (180°C). Line the mini cupcake trays with paper liners. Set the prepared trays aside.

3. In a large bowl, and using an electric stand mixer fitted with a paddle attachment, beat the cake mix, pudding mix, water, oil and eggs on medium speed for 2 to 3 minutes, or until well blended. Scrape the sides of the bowl and mix again until all the ingredients are incorporated.

4. Using a cookie scoop, fill each paper liner with batter to fill the liner (about two-thirds full, dividing evenly between the cupcake trays.

5. Bake the cupcakes for 10–13 minutes, or until a toothpick inserted into the center comes out clean, or the tops spring back when lightly touched. Remove the cupcakes from the oven and place the trays on wire cooling racks for 5 minutes. Take the cupcakes out of the trays and allow them to cool completely on wire racks before decorating.

6. Meanwhile, make the one batch of buttercream frosting.

7. Add turquoise food coloring to the frosting until it reaches the desired shade. Place the #1M Wilton decorating tip inside the pastry bag (no need to use a coupler) and fill with the frosting.

8. To decorate the cupcakes, hold the pastry bag in an upright position and squeeze the bag while turning clockwise, to make a large swirly rosette. Place a pink candy baby bottle on each cupcake.

Stork Delivery Bites

WRAPPED IN A BOW, THESE CANDY-COVERED PEANUT BUTTER BALLS ARE A GREAT EXAMPLE
OF A TRUFFLE MADE SIMPLE. TRY ADDING CHOPPED PEANUTS TO THE MIXTURE
IF YOU LIKE A LITTLE CRUNCH.

MAKES 40 BITES

INGREDIENTS

1 (12-OUNCE [340 G]) PACKAGE PINK
CANDY MELTS

1 (16-OUNCE [453 G]) PACKAGE NUTTER
BUTTER COOKIES, FINELY CRUSHED

1 (8-OUNCE [225 G] PACKAGE CREAM
CHEESE, SOFTENED

2 (12-OUNCE [340 G]) PACKAGES WHITE
CANDY MELTS

YOU WILL NEED

PLASTIC CANDY MOLD FOR SMALL PINK
BOW DECORATIONS

WAXED PAPER

40 MINI PAPER CUPCAKE LINERS

DISPOSABLE PASTRY BAG

DIRECTIONS

1. Melt the pink candy melts in a microwave-safe bowl in 30-second increments at 40% power for about 1½ minutes, stirring as needed until smooth. Pour melted candy into disposable pastry bag and trim tip with scissors. Fill the candy mold with the melted candy and chill until set, about 30 minutes. Remove the candies from the mold and set aside.

2. In a large bowl, and using a large wooden spoon, mix the cream cheese and crushed Nutter Butter cookies until well blended. Roll into tablespoon-size balls. Chill for about 1 hour.

3. Melt the white candy melts in a microwave-safe bowl in 30-second increments at 40% power for about 1½ to 2 minutes, stirring as needed until smooth. Using a fork, dip the balls into the melted white candy, and lay on waxed paper to dry completely.

4. Fasten pink candy bows to the bites with a dab of melted candy, and place the bites in mini paper cupcake liners to serve.

Bitty Banana Pudding Cups

THESE TIMELESS PUDDING TREATS ARE EVEN MORE CHARMING SERVED IN GLASS BABY FOOD JARS. I WANTED TO INCORPORATE THE COLOR YELLOW ON MY TABLE, SO I CHOSE BANANA-FLAVORED PUDDING, BUT ANY FLAVORED PUDDING IS GREAT. JUST ATTACH A WOODEN SPOON WITH YELLOW RIBBON TO MAKE THIS PUDDING TREAT POP.

MAKES 15 TO 18 PUDDING CUPS

INGREDIENTS

2 (3.4-OUNCE [110 G]) BOXES JELL-O INSTANT BANANA CREAM PUDDING AND PIE FILLING

1 (12-OUNCE [340 G]) BOX MINI NILLA WAFERS

YOU WILL NEED

GLASS BABY FOOD JARS, OR SIMILAR CONTAINERS

WOODEN SPOONS

YELLOW RIBBON

DIRECTIONS

1. Prepare the instant banana pudding mix according to the package directions. Chill for about 30 minutes.

2. When ready to serve, place a handful of Nilla Wafers in the bottom of the jars (about six mini cookies), spoon some pudding on top. Repeat with more cookies, ending with a final layer of pudding.

3. Fasten the wooden spoons to the sides of the jars with yellow ribbon tied in a bow.

Rattles from Seattle

YOU'LL BE SURPRISED HOW SIMPLE THESE LITTLE RATTLES ARE TO MAKE AND HOW GREAT THEY TASTE. STORE-BOUGHT OREO COOKIES ARE DIPPED IN VANILLA CANDY MELTS, SPRINKLED, AND TIED WITH A BOW. STAND THEM IN STYROFOAM COVERED IN NOSTALGIC BABY SHOWER MINTS.

MAKES 24 POPS

INGREDIENTS

1 (14.3-OUNCE [405 G]) PACKAGE OREO COOKIES

2 (12-OUNCE [340 G]) PACKAGES WHITE CANDY MELTS

PASTEL STAR SPRINKLES

YOU WILL NEED

STYROFOAM

24 PINK AND WHITE STRIPED STRAWS

24 PIECES BLUE RIBBON

DIRECTIONS

1. Melt the candy melts in a microwave-safe bowl in 30-second increments at 40% power for about 1 ½ to 2 minutes, stirring as needed until smooth.

2. Insert paper straws into the middle of oreo cookies.

3. Dip the Oreos into the melted candy and decorate the bottom half of each with pastel star sprinkles while still tacky. Stand the Oreo Rattles up in a sheet of Styrofoam to dry.

4. Tie bows around the straws with blue ribbon.

She's Going to Pop Corn!

MOMS-TO-BE OFTEN CRAVE A SWEET AND SALTY SNACK. I KNOW I DID WHEN I WAS PREGNANT. MIX UP THIS FUN BLEND OF SWEET AND SALTY SNACKS BY ADDING VARIOUS MINIATURE CANDY PIECES OR DRIZZLING MILK CHOCOLATE INSTEAD OF VANILLA CANDY.

MAKES APPROXIMATELY 15 CUPS

INGREDIENTS

2 (2.9-OUNCE [82 G]) BAGS ORVILLE REDENBACHER'S SALTY AND SWEET KETTLE KORN

1 (12-OUNCE [340 G]) PACKAGE PINK CANDY MELTS

1 (12-OUNCE [340 G]) PACKAGE BLUE CANDY MELTS

1 (8-OUNCE [226 G]) BAG MINI SNICKERS BITES

ABOUT 8 OUNCES (225 G) MINI PRETZEL TWISTS

PASTEL SPRINKLES

YOU WILL NEED

WAXED PAPER

DIRECTIONS

1. Pop the microwave popcorn according to the package directions. Lay flat on waxed paper to cool.

2. Lay snickers bites on waxed paper.

3. Melt the pink and blue candy melts in separate microwave-safe bowls in 30-second increments at 40% power for about 1½ minutes, stirring as needed until smooth. Drizzle the pink candy over the popcorn and Snickers, sprinkling with pastel sprinkles while the candy is still tacky.

4. Dip one half side of the pretzels in the blue candy. Lay flat on waxed paper to set.

5. Mix all the ingredients together in a large bowl and serve.

Vintage Baby Jenny Cookies

MOMS-TO-BE LOVE TO SEE THEIR BABY'S NAME. PERSONALIZE THESE BABY SHOWER COOKIES BY DRAWING BABY'S NAME OR INITIALS ON THE BIB COOKIES. DECORATE BOTTLE TOPS, BABY BUGGIES AND RATTLES IN COLORS TO MATCH YOUR THEME.

IF YOU WISH TO MAKE ALL FIVE SUGAR COOKIES ON THE BABY DESSERT TABLE AS THEY'RE PICTURED, MAKE ONE BATCH OF BUTTERCREAM FROSTING AS DIRECTED ON PAGE 10 AND DIVIDE AND TINT EACH WITH THE APPROPRIATE COLORS. ATTACH #4 WILTON DECORATING TIPS AND COUPLERS TO EACH OF THE PASTRY BAGS AND FILL WITH FROSTING; ONE WITH WHITE FROSTING, BLUE, YELLOW, AND PINK. YOU'LL BE MAKING ONE BATCH OF SUGAR COOKIE DOUGH AND USING IT FOR ALL FOUR COOKIE SHAPES. SEE PAGE 12 IN THE "BASICS" CHAPTER FOR THE COOKIE INGREDIENTS AND DIRECTIONS.

MAKES ABOUT 24 COOKIES

YOU WILL NEED

ROLLING PIN
2 NONSTICK COOKIE SHEETS
COOKIE SPATULA
RATTLE COOKIE CUTTER
BABY CARRIAGE COOKIE CUTTER
BABY BOTTLE COOKIE CUTTER
BABY BIB COOKIE CUTTER
5 DISPOSABLE PASTRY BAGS
¼ CUP (55 G) VANILLA CANDY MELTS
4 #4 WILTON DECORATING TIPS
4 WILTON COUPLERS
AMERICOLOR SOFT GEL PASTE COLORS TO MAKE YELLOW, BLUE AND PINK

Rattle Cookies

INGREDIENTS

PINK BUTTERCREAM
BLUE BUTTERCREAM
YELLOW BUTTERCREAM
WHITE BUTTERCREAM
ROUND PASTEL SPRINKLES

To decorate the rattle cookies, use the pastry bag filled with pink frosting, and fitted with a #4 Wilton decorating tip, outline the top and bottom circles of three to four of the rattle cookies. Fill in the outlines with pink frosting, running it horizontally from one side to the other until they are completely filled in. Repeat with the blue, yellow and white frosting, outlining and filling in three to four cookies with each color. Sprinkle the bottom half of the bottom circles with pastel sprinkles, pressing lightly to adhere. Using the pastry bag with white frosting, draw a bow around the middle of each rattle.

(continued)

Baby Buggy Cookies

INGREDIENTS
WHITE BUTTERCREAM
BLUE BUTTERCREAM
PINK BUTTERCREAM

To decorate the baby buggy cookies, use the pastry bag filled with pink frosting, and fitted with a #4 Wilton decorating tip, outline all the buggies including the handles, but avoiding the wheels. Using the bag with white frosting, fill in the hoods, following the curves. Fill in half the buggy bottoms with blue frosting and half with pink frosting, running it horizontally from one side to the other until they are completely filled in. Using the same blue and pink frosting, draw three ribs on each hood as shown in the photo. Using the bag with white frosting, draw wheels and spokes, as well as a scalloped decoration across each buggy where the two colors of the buggy bottom and hood meet. Give each wheel a pink or blue hubcap.

Baby Bottle Cookies

INGREDIENTS
PINK BUTTERCREAM
YELLOW BUTTERCREAM
BLUE BUTTERCREAM
WHITE BUTTERCREAM

To decorate the baby bottle cookies, use the pastry bag filled with white frosting, and fitted with a #4 Wilton decorating tip, outline all the bottles, except the caps and nipples. Fill in the bottles with white frosting, running it horizontally from one side to the other until they are completely filled in. Using the pastry bag filled with blue frosting, draw measurement lines on half the bottles, and a ring around the neck. Using the pink frosting, repeat with the remainder of the bottles, also drawing rings around the top. Draw a yellow nipple at the top of each bottle.

Baby Bib Cookies

INGREDIENTS
PINK BUTTERCREAM
YELLOW BUTTERCREAM
BLUE BUTTERCREAM
WHITE BUTTERCREAM

YOU WILL NEED
PINK RIBBONS

Before decorating your cookies with buttercream, first attach the strings of the bib. Tie small bows from pink ribbon. Melt ¼ cup (55 g) of candy melts in microwave for about 30 seconds at 40% power or until melted in disposable pastry bag. Once melted, cut small tip and attach bib strings using melted candy to the back of each cookie. To decorate the baby bib cookies, use the pastry bag filled with pink frosting, and fitted with a #4 Wilton decorating tip, outline one-third of the cookies. Fill in the outlines with pink frosting, running it horizontally from one side to the other until they are completely filled in. Repeat with the blue and yellow frosting, outlining and filling in one third of each of the remaining cookies with each color. Using the pastry bag filled with white frosting, decorate each cookie a little different. Draw "Baby" on a few cookies, draw polka dots on some and little flowers on others with yellow frosting.

5

Spring Garden

ONE AFTERNOON A FEW YEARS AGO, I WAS FINISHING UP A BAKING ORDER AND HAD ABOUT A DOZEN ROUND SUGAR COOKIES LEFT OVER, SITTING NAKED ON MY TABLE. I ALSO HAD AN ICING BAG FILLED WITH YELLOW BUTTERCREAM AND A 1M TIP. I DECIDED TO SEE HOW A COOKIE WOULD LOOK IF I DECORATED IT LIKE A CUPCAKE. THE SUGAR COOKIES WERE ABOUT THE SAME DIAMETER OF THE CUPCAKE TOP—IT WAS JUST CRAZY ENOUGH TO WORK.

I ICED THE COOKIE, SQUEEZING MY BAG AND LAYERING UNTIL I REACHED THE TOP. IT LOOKED LIKE A HOT MESS, OVERLOADED WITH ICING. I TRIED AGAIN WITH ANOTHER COOKIE, THIS TIME STARTING IN THE MIDDLE AND WORKING MY WAY OUT. AS I ROUNDED THE LAST SWIRL, I REALIZED I HAD JUST CREATED WHAT LOOKED LIKE A ROSE. IT WAS GORGEOUS, AND IT TOOK ABOUT THREE SECONDS TO DECORATE. I FINISHED THE REST OF THE COOKIES AS "YELLOW ROSES" AND COULDN'T WAIT TO TRY THIS TECHNIQUE AGAIN. I TRIED IT ON CUPCAKES AND DISCOVERED IT WAS JUST AS PRETTY, JUST AS SIMPLE AND INSANELY FAST.

People loved the "rose" cookies, so I started using them on cakes. I'd had a client who was having an intimate wedding ceremony and needed a small cutting cake for the reception. They had ordered cake pops and cupcakes for the guests, but wanted something special for the two of them to cut into. This was the perfect opportunity to try my new rose technique on a cake. I baked a small, 6-inch (15 cm) double layer cake and gave it a crumb coat. After letting it crust, I filled my decorating bag with white buttercream and a 1M tip. Starting at the base of the cake, I began making roses up the sides of the cake. It seemed to be working. As I spun my cake turntable, embellishing the cake with rose after rose, I realized it was beautiful. With a little imagination, my first chic buttercream cake had been created—sparking a frenzy that lasted all summer. With just a switch of food coloring, the rose cake could work for any palette and theme.

That's the beauty of it: You can experiment with other cupcake and cookie decorating tips to create other textures. I discovered a 2D tip would cover my cake with buttercream petals, a 104 tip would create ruffles, and any petal tip would make a ribbon texture, either vertically or horizontally. (For more tip design information, see the Basics chapter.) These elegant buttercream cakes are simple, delicious and look like you spent hours making them.

SETTING THE TABLE

Use a shabby, weathered wood table as your base. Multicolor glass and milk cake stands can line the table in random order. I found an old wooden children's chair and mint-colored wood stepstool that added interest, height and color. Try filling vintage galvanized watering cans with flowers and placing them around the table. Then bring out the desserts.

Decorate with assorted treats shaped and flavored in spring themes. Normally, I like to use a cake as my table centerpiece, but for my spring table, I decided to make three, using the various buttercream textured decorating techniques and flavoring them with lemon, carrot cake and yellow cake. I gave the cupcakes bunny ear cookie toppers, shaped Rice Krispie treats into flowers, and baked sugar cookies into the shape of a garden carrot. I sprinkled cake pops in an assortment of pastel sanding sugars, and—my favorite—I made cupcakes inside miniature terra-cotta pots and decorated them to look like hydrangeas. The table has a variety of flavors and colors, adaptable for any spring occasion.

SPRING GARDEN DESSERTS

- ♥ **Green Swirl Ribbon Cake**
- ♥ **Yellow Petal Cake**
- ♥ **Pink Rose Cake**
- ♥ **Bunny Ear Cupcakes**
- ♥ **Hydrangea Flower Pot Cupcakes**
- ♥ **Lemon Bloom Cake Pops**
- ♥ **Flower Rice Krispie Treats**
- ♥ **Brownie Nests**
- ♥ **Pink and Purple Flower Cookies**
- ♥ **Yellow Rose Cookies**
- ♥ **Garden Carrot Cookies**

Green Swirl Ribbon Cake

THIS PASTEL GREEN SWIRL RIBBON CAKE IS SIMILAR TO THE RED VELVET RIBBON CAKE IN THE "DOWN ON THE FARM" CHAPTER AS FAR AS THE DECORATING TECHNIQUE, BUT IT HAS ITS OWN PERSONALITY. USE A TOTALLY DIFFERENT COLOR FROSTING—PASTEL GREEN INSTEAD OF BRIGHT RED—AND USE A DIFFERENT DECORATING TIP TO CREATE THE SOFT LOVELY RIBBONS. THIS LEMONY CAKE LOOKS LIKE YOU SPENT ALL DAY DECORATING IT, BUT THE PASTEL GREEN RIBBONS SEEM TO FLOW EFFORTLESSLY FROM THE PASTRY BAG ON THEIR OWN.

Note: If you have anything smaller than a 6-quart (6.7 L) mixer, you may need to mix the cake batter in two batches.

MAKES ONE 6-INCH (15 CM) AND 8-INCH (20.5 CM) TIERED CAKE

INGREDIENTS

COOKING SPRAY OR CRISCO OR BUTTER PLUS FLOUR, FOR PANS

3 (18.25-OUNCE [517 G]) BOXES DUNCAN HINES LEMON CAKE MIX

3 (3.4-OUNCE [110 G]) BOXES JELL-O LEMON INSTANT PUDDING AND PIE FILLING, DRY

3 CUPS (710 ML) WATER

1 CUP (235 ML) OIL

12 LARGE EGGS

3 BATCHES BUTTERCREAM FROSTING (PAGE 10)

AMERICOLOR MINT GREEN SOFT GEL PASTE COLOR

DIRECTIONS

1. Preheat the oven to 350°F (180°C). Coat the 8-inch (20.5 cm) and 6-inch (15 cm) round nonstick cake pans with cooking spray, or grease and flour the pans, tapping out the excess flour. Set the prepared pans aside.

2. In a large bowl, and using an electric stand mixer fitted with a paddle attachment, beat the cake mix, pudding mix, water, oil and eggs on medium speed for 2 to 3 minutes, or until well blended. Scrape the sides of the bowl and mix again until all the ingredients are incorporated.

3. Pour the batter into the prepared cake pans, filling each one approximately three-quarters full.

4. Place the pans in the preheated oven, on the middle rack. Bake the 6-inch (15 cm) cakes for 25 to 30 minutes, and the 8-inch (20.5 cm) cakes for 30 to 35 minutes, or until a toothpick inserted into the center comes out clean.

5. Remove the pans from the oven and place on wire cooling racks for 25 to 30 minutes. Run a knife around the edges of the cakes, flip the pans over and gently extract the cakes. Return the cakes to the wire racks and finish cooling completely before frosting and decorating. After the layers are cooled, freeze or refrigerate the cakes for 1 hour before decorating to reduce crumbs and make for a smoother icing process.

6. Meanwhile, make the three batches of buttercream frosting. Add green food coloring to the frosting until it reaches the desired shade.

2 (8 × 2-INCH (20.5 × 5 CM]) AND
2 (6 × 2-INCH [15 × 5 CM]) ROUND
NONSTICK CAKE PANS

CAKE CUTTER OR LONG, SERRATED
KNIFE

2 ROUND CARDBOARD OR PLASTIC
CAKE BOARDS

OFFSET ANGLED SPATULA

LARGE PASTRY BAG

#18 WILTON DECORATING TIP

WILTON COUPLER

5 (¼-INCH [6 MM])-THICK) DOWELS OR
THICK PLASTIC STRAWS

LARGE, FLAT SPATULA

CAKE DECORATING TURNTABLE

LARGE DECORATING SPATULA

TO ASSEMBLE AND DECORATE THE CAKE

1. Before decorating, trim the crowns from the cake tops with a cake cutter or long, serrated knife so they are flat and even.

2. Place one of the 8-inch (20.5 cm) cakes on a cake board. Using the angled cake spatula, spread about ½ cup (120 ml) of frosting evenly across the top of the cake layer. Place the second 8-inch (20.5 cm) cake on top of the first, with the cut side on the bottom. Use the angled cake spatula to cover the cake completely with a very thin layer of icing (or crumb coat) to help reduce the amount of crumbs in the final coat of icing. Set the two-tiered, 8-inch (20.5 cm) cake aside.

3. Repeat this process with the 6-inch (15 cm) cake layers, using another ½ cup (120 ml) of buttercream frosting between the layers, and icing the sides and top of the cake. Once the same process has been completed on the 6-inch (15 cm) cake layers, allow them to dry for 1 hour, or until the icing crusts.

4. Attach Wilton decorating tip #18 and the coupler to the pastry bag and fill with green frosting. Set aside.

5. Create supports for the smaller cake to sit atop the larger cake by placing the dowels into the top of the 8-inch (20.5 cm) cake. Insert the first dowel into the cake and use a pen to mark the dowel at the point where it just comes to the top of the cake. Remove the dowel and cut it at that mark. Cut three to four additional dowels or straws to the same length and place them in a circle, approximately 2 inches (5 cm) from the center of the cake, and evenly spaced. Using a large, flat spatula, carefully center and place the 6-inch (15 cm) tier on top of the 8-inch (20.5 cm) tier.

6. Place the cake on a rotating cake turntable. Using a large decorating spatula, frost the top of the cake smooth. Using the pastry bag filled with green frosting and fitted with a #18 decorating tip, hold the bag vertically, and starting at the bottom of the cake, squeeze the pastry bag while going back and forth overlapping in short (1-inch [2.5 cm]-wide) rows while you go up the side of the cake tier. Continue overlapping the vertical ribbons; start again at the bottom of the cake right next to the first row, and repeat the process all the way to the top edge of the 8-inch (20.5 cm) tier. Repeat this until both tiers are full of vertical ribbon swirls.

Pink Rose Cake

THE ELEGANT PINK ROSES ON THIS PRETTY-IN-PINK CAKE HIDE A DELICIOUS SURPRISE: WHEN YOU SLICE INTO IT, YOU'RE GREETED WITH A SUBTLE WHIFF OF PINEAPPLE AND SPICES. THE BEAUTIFUL ROSES ON THE OUTSIDE ONLY LOOK DIFFICULT BUT ARE EASILY DONE WITH A STAR TIP AND SIMPLE CLOCKWISE WRIST MOTIONS. WITH A LITTLE PRACTICE, YOU'LL HAVE CREATED A STUNNING SPRING CENTERPIECE.

Makes one 8-inch (20.5 cm) layer cake

INGREDIENTS

COOKING SPRAY OR CRISCO OR BUTTER PLUS FLOUR, FOR PANS

1 (18.25-OUNCE [517 G])BOX DUNCAN HINES CARROT CAKE MIX

1 CUP (235 ML) WATER

¼ CUP (60 ML) OIL

4 LARGE EGGS

1 (8-OUNCE [225 G]) CAN CRUSHED PINEAPPLE WITH JUICE

1 FRESH CARROT, GRATED

½ CUP (75 G) WALNUTS, FINELY CHOPPED

2 BATCHES BUTTERCREAM FROSTING (PAGE 10)

AMERICOLOR PINK SOFT GEL PASTE COLOR

DIRECTIONS

1. Preheat the oven to 350°F (180°C). Coat the 8-inch (20.5 cm) round nonstick cake pans with cooking spray, or grease and flour the pans, tapping out the excess flour. Set the prepared pans aside.

2. In a large bowl, and using an electric stand mixer fitted with a paddle attachment, beat the cake mix, water, oil and eggs on medium speed for 2 to 3 minutes, or until well blended. Add the pineapple and grated carrot and mix again just until all the ingredients are incorporated, scraping the sides of the bowl as needed. Fold in the walnuts.

3. Pour the batter into the prepared cake pans, dividing the batter equally between the two pans.

4. Place the pans in the preheated oven, on the middle rack. Bake the cake layers for 37 to 42 minutes, or until a toothpick inserted into the center comes out clean.

5. Remove the pans from the oven and place on wire cooling racks for 25 to 30 minutes. Run a knife around the edges of the cakes, flip the pans over and gently extract the cakes. Return the cakes to the wire racks and finish cooling completely before frosting and decorating. After layers are cooled, freeze or refrigerate the cakes for 1 hour before decorating to reduce crumbs and make for a smoother icing process.

6. Meanwhile, make the two batches of buttercream frosting. Add pink food coloring to the frosting until it reaches the desired shade.

YOU WILL NEED

2 (8 × 2-INCH [20.5 × 5 CM]) ROUND
NONSTICK CAKE PANS

CAKE CUTTER OR LONG, SERRATED
KNIFE

1 ROUND CARDBOARD OR PLASTIC
CAKE BOARD

OFFSET ANGLED SPATULA

CAKE DECORATING TURNTABLE

LARGE PASTRY BAG

#1M WILTON DECORATING TIP

TO ASSEMBLE AND DECORATE THE CAKE

1. Before decorating, trim the crowns from the cake tops with a cake cutter or long, serrated knife so they are flat and even.

2. Place one of the 8-inch (20.5 cm) layers on a cake board cut side up. Using the angled cake spatula, spread about ½ cup (120 ml) of buttercream evenly across the top of the cake layer. Place the second 8-inch (20.5 cm) layer on top of the first, pressing down lightly. Use the angled cake spatula to cover the cake completely with a very thin layer of pink frosting (or crumb coat) to help reduce the amount of crumbs in the final coat of icing. Set the cake aside and allow it to dry for 1 hour, or until the icing crusts.

3. Place the cake on the rotating cake turntable. Using a large decorating spatula, frost the top of the cake smooth.

4. Place the #1M Wilton decorating tip inside the pastry bag (no need to use a coupler) and fill with pink frosting. Hold the bag horizontally and start from the bottom of the cake to create rows of roses. Starting in the middle of the rose, squeeze the pastry bag and make a few spirals in a counterclockwise motion around the center, ending at the top of the rose. Don't worry if you end the rose with a few tails. These will be covered by the next row of roses. Turn the turntable and make another rose following the same technique, always ending at the top of the rose. Continue all the way around the cake until you meet up with the first rose you created.

5. Continue with the second row of roses, slightly touching the roses on the bottom row so there are no gaps or tails showing until you reach the top of the cake.

6. Starting at the outside edge on the top of the cake, create a circle of roses. Repeat with a second circle of roses inside the first, and continue until the top of the cake is covered in roses.

Yellow Petal Cake

THIS GORGEOUS YELLOW PETAL CAKE'S DECORATION TECHNIQUE IS EXTREMELY FORGIVING. THERE'S NO NEED FOR PERFECT STARS OR STRAIGHT LINES—THAT'S WHAT MAKES IT SO SIMPLE AND IRRESISTIBLE.

MAKES ONE 4-INCH (10 CM) AND 6-INCH (15 CM) TIERED CAKE

INGREDIENTS

COOKING SPRAY OR CRISCO OR BUTTER PLUS FLOUR, FOR PANS

2 (18.25-OUNCE [517 G]) BOXES DUNCAN HINES YELLOW CAKE MIX

2 (3.4-OUNCE [110 G]) BOXES JELL-O VANILLA INSTANT PUDDING AND PIE FILLING, DRY

2 CUPS (475 ML) WATER

⅔ CUP (157 ML) OIL

8 LARGE EGGS

2 BATCHES BUTTERCREAM FROSTING (PAGE 10)

AMERICOLOR YELLOW SOFT GEL PASTE COLOR

YOU WILL NEED

2 (6 × 2-INCH [15 × 5 CM]) AND 2 (4 × 2-INCH [10 × 5 CM]) ROUND NONSTICK CAKE PANS

CAKE CUTTER OR LONG, SERRATED KNIFE

2 ROUND CARDBOARD OR PLASTIC CAKE BOARDS

OFFSET ANGLED SPATULA

LARGE PASTRY BAG

#2D WILTON DECORATING TIP

3 (¼-INCH [6 MM]-THICK) DOWELS OR THICK PLASTIC STRAWS

CAKE DECORATING TURNTABLE

DIRECTIONS

1. Preheat the oven to 350°F (180°C). Coat the 4-inch (10 cm) and 6-inch (15 cm) round nonstick cake pans with cooking spray, or grease and flour the pans, tapping out the excess flour. Set the prepared pans aside.

2. In a large bowl, and using an electric stand mixer fitted with a paddle attachment, beat the cake mix, pudding mix, water, oil and eggs on medium speed for 2 to 3 minutes, or until well blended. Scrape the sides of the bowl and mix again until all the ingredients are incorporated.

3. Pour batter into the prepared cake pans, filling each one approximately three-quarters full.

4. Place the pans in the preheated oven, on the middle rack. Bake 4-inch (10 cm) cakes for 20 to 25 minutes, and 6-inch (15 cm) cakes for 25 to 30 minutes, or until a toothpick inserted into the center comes out clean.

5. Remove the pans from the oven and place on wire cooling racks for 25 to 30 minutes. Run a knife around the edges of the cakes, flip the pans over and gently extract the cakes. Return the cakes to the wire racks and finish cooling completely before frosting and decorating. After the layers are cooled, freeze or refrigerate the cakes for 1 hour before decorating to reduce crumbs and make for a smoother icing process.

6. Meanwhile, make the two batches of buttercream frosting. Add yellow food coloring to the frosting until it reaches the desired shade.

TO ASSEMBLE AND DECORATE THE CAKE

1. Before decorating, trim the crowns from the cake tops with a cake cutter or long, serrated knife so they are flat and even.

2. Place one of the 6-inch (15 cm) cakes on a cake board. Using the angled cake spatula, spread about ½ cup (120 ml) frosting evenly across the top of the cake layer. Place the second 6-inch (15 cm) cake on top of the first, with the cut side on the bottom. Use the angled cake spatula to cover the cake completely with a very thin layer of icing (or crumb coat) to help reduce the amount of crumbs in the final coat of icing. Set the two-tiered 6-inch (15 cm) cake aside.

3. Repeat this process with the 4-inch (10 cm) cake layers, using another ⅓ cup (80 ml) of buttercream frosting between the layers, and icing the sides and top of the cake. Once the same process has been completed on the 4-inch (10 cm) cake layers, allow them to dry for 1 hour, or until the icing crusts.

4. Place the #2D Wilton decorating tip inside the pastry bag (no need to use a coupler) and fill with yellow frosting. Set aside.

5. Create supports for the smaller cake to sit atop the larger cake by placing the dowels into the top of the 6-inch (15 cm) cake. Insert the first dowel into the cake and use a pen to mark the dowel at the point where it just comes to the top of the cake. Remove the dowel and cut it at that mark. Cut 3 additional dowels or straws to the same length and place them in a circle, approximately 2 inches from the center of the cake, and evenly spaced. Using a large flat spatula, carefully center and place the 4-inch (10 cm) tier on top of the 6-inch (15 cm) cake tier.

6. Place the cake on a rotating cake turntable. Using a large decorating spatula, frost the top of the cake for a nice smooth finish. Using the pastry bag filled with yellow frosting, begin at the bottom of your cake. Squeeze the pastry bag to make a star shape. Continue around base of cake, spinning your turntable as you go. Just keep making stars around the base of the cake moving up, covering all sides and bases with yellow buttercream stars.

Bunny Ear Cupcakes

THE BEST THING ABOUT THESE CUPCAKES? THEY'RE TWO DESSERTS IN ONE—A DELICIOUSLY MOIST CUPCAKE AND ONE OF MY BUTTERY SUGAR COOKIES DECORATED WITH FLUFFY WHITE BUTTERCREAM FROSTING.

Note: These cupcakes are made with simple white cake, but there's no reason you can't experiment with different flavorings inside. Try adding a teaspoon of lemon, raspberry or strawberry extract while mixing the cake batter. You could even add some flavoring to the buttercream frosting to match the cupcake's flavor.

MAKES 24 STANDARD CUPCAKES

INGREDIENTS

1 (18.25-OUNCE [517 G]) BOX DUNCAN HINES WHITE CAKE MIX

1 (3.4-OUNCE [110 G]) BOX JELL-O VANILLA INSTANT PUDDING AND PIE FILLING, DRY

1 CUP (235 ML) WATER

⅓ CUP (80 ML) OIL

4 LARGE EGGS

2 BATCHES BUTTERCREAM FROSTING (PAGE 10)

24 DECORATED BUNNY EAR COOKIES (PAGE 12)

YOU WILL NEED

2 STANDARD-SIZE CUPCAKE TRAYS

24 STANDARD PAPER CUPCAKE LINERS

SMALL COOKIE SCOOP

1 DISPOSABLE PASTRY BAG

WILTON TIP 1 A OR ATECO 800 (BOTH ARE OVERSIZE ROUND TIPS)

BUNNY COOKIE CUTTER

DIRECTIONS

1. Preheat the oven to 350°F (180°C). Line the cupcake trays with paper cupcake liners. Set the prepared pans aside.

2. In a large bowl, and using an electric stand mixer fitted with a paddle attachment, beat the cake mix, pudding mix, water, oil and eggs on medium speed for 2 to 3 minutes, or until well blended. Scrape down the sides of the bowl, and mix again until all the ingredients are incorporated.

3. Using a cookie scoop, fill each paper liner with batter to fill the liner about two-thirds full, dividing evenly between the cupcake trays.

4. Bake the cupcakes for 18 to 20 minutes, or until a toothpick inserted into the center comes out clean, or the tops spring back when lightly touched. Remove the cupcakes from the oven and place the trays on wire cooling racks for 15 minutes. Take the cupcakes out of the trays and allow them to cool completely on wire racks before decorating.

5. Make two batches of buttercream frosting.

6. To decorate the cupcakes place the #1A Wilton or #800 Ateco decorating tip inside the pastry bag (no need to use a coupler) and fill with white frosting. Holding the pastry bag in an upright position, squeeze the bag while going clockwise, to make a large swirl.

7. To decorate, stand one bunny ear cookie into the top of each cupcake.

Hydrangea Flower Pot Cupcakes

MY GUESTS ALWAYS LOVE THESE VIBRANTLY COLORED TERRA-COTTA FLOWERPOTS OVERFLOWING WITH BLUE, LIFELIKE HYDRANGEAS. AND NO ONE WILL GUESS THERE'S A MOIST DEVIL'S FOOD CUPCAKE HIDDEN BENEATH ALL THOSE BLUE BUTTERCREAM FLOWERS.

MAKES 48 MINI CUPCAKES

INGREDIENTS

1 (18.25OUNCE [517 G]) BOX DUNCAN HINES DEVIL'S FOOD CAKE MIX

1 (3.4-OUNCE [110 G]) BOX JELL-O CHOCOLATE INSTANT PUDDING AND PIE FILLING, DRY

1 CUP (235 ML) WATER

⅓ CUP (80 ML) OIL

4 LARGE EGGS

1 BATCH BUTTERCREAM FROSTING (PAGE 10)

AMERICOLOR SKY BLUE SOFT GEL PASTE COLOR

YOU WILL NEED

2 MINI CUPCAKE TRAYS

48 MINI PAPER CUPCAKE LINERS

SMALL COOKIE SCOOP

DISPOSABLE PASTRY BAG

#2D WILTON DECORATING TIP

48 MINI TERRA-COTTA POTS, FOUND ON ANY CRAFT STORE'S FLORAL AISLE

DIRECTIONS

1. Preheat the oven to 350°F (180°C). Line the mini cupcake trays with paper liners. Set the prepared trays aside.

2. In a large bowl, and using an electric stand mixer fitted with a paddle attachment, beat the cake mix, pudding mix, water, oil and eggs on medium speed for 2 to 3 minutes, or until well blended. Scrape the sides of the bowl and mix again until all the ingredients are incorporated.

3. Using a cookie scoop, fill each paper liner with batter to fill the liner (about two-thirds full, dividing evenly between the cupcake trays.

4. Bake the cupcakes for 10-13 minutes, or until a toothpick inserted into the center comes out clean, or the tops spring back when lightly touched. Remove the cupcakes from the oven and place the trays on wire cooling racks for 5 minutes. Take the cupcakes out of the trays and allow them to cool completely on the wire racks before decorating.

5. Meanwhile, make the one batch of buttercream frosting.

6. Add blue food coloring to the frosting until it reaches the desired shade. Place the #2D Wilton decorating tip inside the pastry bag (no need to use a coupler) and fill with frosting. Set aside.

7. To decorate the cupcakes, hold the pastry bag in an upright position, and squeeze while twisting wrist clockwise and dotting hydrangea blooms to cover the top of each cupcake. Put cupcakes in flower pot when done decorating.

Lemon Bloom Cake Pops

THE BEST THING ABOUT SPRING IS THE BEAUTIFUL PASTEL COLORS THAT SEEM TO POP OUT EVERYWHERE. THESE WHITE-CHOCOLATE-DIPPED, LEMONY CAKE POPS ATOP BRIGHTLY COLORED STRAWS ARE SPRINKLED WITH PINK, YELLOW AND MINT GREEN PASTEL SANDING SUGAR. YOU CAN'T HELP BUT POP MORE THAN ONE.

MAKES 40 CAKE POPS

INGREDIENTS

COOKING SPRAY OR CRISCO OR BUTTER PLUS FLOUR, FOR PANS

1 (18.25-OUNCE [517 G]) BOX DUNCAN HINES LEMON CAKE MIX

1 (3.4-OUNCE [110 G]) BOX JELL-O LEMON INSTANT PUDDING AND PIE FILLING, DRY

1 CUP (235 ML) WATER

⅓ CUP (80 ML) OIL

4 LARGE EGGS

½ TO ¾ CUP (120 TO 175 ML) BUTTERCREAM FROSTING (PAGE 10)

3 (12-OUNCE [340 G]) PACKAGES WHITE CANDY MELTS

GREEN SANDING SUGAR

PINK SANDING SUGAR

YELLOW SANDING SUGAR

BLUE SANDING SUGAR

YOU WILL NEED

9 × 13-INCH (23 × 33 CM) BAKING PAN OR CASSEROLE DISH

40 PASTEL LOLLIPOP STICKS

STYROFOAM

DIRECTIONS

1. Preheat the oven to 350°F (180°C). Coat the 9 × 13-inch (23 × 33 cm) baking pan with cooking spray, or grease and flour the pan, tapping out excess flour. Set aside.

2. In a large bowl, and using an electric stand mixer fitted with a paddle attachment, beat the cake mix, pudding mix, water, oil and eggs on medium speed for 2 to 3 minutes, or until well blended. Scrape the sides of the bowl and mix again until all the ingredients are incorporated.

3. Pour the batter into the prepared cake pan. Place the pan in the preheated oven, and bake for 35 to 40 minutes, or until a toothpick inserted into the center comes out clean.

4. Remove the pan from the oven and place on a wire cooling rack for 25 to 30 minutes. Let cool completely before making the cake pops.

5. Mash up the cake and place in a large bowl. Using an electric stand mixer fitted with a paddle attachment, mix the cake, ½ to ¾ cup (120 to 175 ml) of icing on medium speed until moist and well blended and the mixture can be molded into a ball.

6. Measure and roll mixture into tablespoon-size balls, and place on a cookie sheet. Refrigerate for 1 hour or until firm.

7. Melt the candy melts in a microwave-safe bowl in 30-second increments at 40% power for about 1½ to 2 minutes, stirring as needed until smooth. Remove the bowl from the microwave.

8. Remove the pops from the refrigerator. Dip each lollipop stick ¼ inch (6 mm) into the melted candy and insert into each cake ball. Proceed to dip each one into the melted white candy. Immediately dust an equal amount of pops with each colored sanding sugar, and stand them up in a sheet of Styrofoam to dry.

Flower Rice Krispie Treats

THIS DESSERT IS SIMPLE AND FUN FOR KIDS TO DECORATE. BRIGHT PURPLE FLOWERS MADE FROM RICE KRISPIE TREATS ARE DIPPED IN PURPLE SPRINKLES AND DECORATED WITH PURPLE M&M'S. WHAT'S NOT TO LOVE?

MAKES 15 TO 18 TREATS

INGREDIENTS

VEGETABLE SPRAY

3 TABLESPOONS (42 G) BUTTER OR MARGARINE

1 (10-OUNCE [280 G]) PACKAGE MINI MARSHMALLOWS (4 CUPS)

AMERICOLOR PURPLE SOFT GEL PASTE COLOR

6 CUPS (150 G) RICE KRISPIES CEREAL

PURPLE SPRINKLES

PURPLE M&MS

YOU WILL NEED

9 × 13-INCH (23 × 33 CM) BAKING PAN OR CASSEROLE DISH

FLOWER COOKIE CUTTER

WAXED PAPER

DIRECTIONS

1. Lightly oil or spray the 9 × 13-inch (23 × 33 cm) baking pan with vegetable spray.

2. In a large saucepan over low heat, melt the butter. Add the marshmallows and stir until melted and smooth. Remove the pan from the heat and add purple food coloring.

3. Add the Rice Krispies and stir until completely coated. Pat into the prepared baking pan and let cool completely to set.

4. Once set, cut out flower shapes, using cookie cutter.

5. Dip the Rice Krispie treats in purple sprinkles and lay flat on waxed paper. Add one M&M in the center of the Rice Krispie flower.

Brownie Nests

EVERYONE LOVES MOIST, CHOCOLATY BROWNIES. MY VERSION IS DRESSED UP WITH BUTTERCREAM FROSTING AND TOPPED WITH TOASTED COCONUT. ADD A FEW JELLY BEANS TO THE TOP, AND SIMPLE BROWNIES TRANSFORM INTO THE SWEETEST ROBIN'S NESTS.

MAKES 30 NESTS

INGREDIENTS

1 CUP (85 G) SWEETENED COCONUT FLAKES

COOKING SPRAY

1 BOX FAMILY-SIZE BROWNIE MIX (MAKE SURE TO ACCOUNT FOR THE INGREDIENTS ON THE BOX)

½ BATCH BUTTERCREAM FROSTING (SEE PAGE 10)

JELLY BEANS

YOU WILL NEED

2 MINI CUPCAKE PANS

DISPOSABLE PASTRY BAG

DIRECTIONS

1. To toast the coconut, spread on a microwave-safe plate. Microwave in 30-second increments at 40% power, gently stirring each time, until the coconut is as brown as you'd like. Set aside to cool.

2. Preheat the oven to 350°F (180°C). Lightly spray the mini cupcake pans with cooking spray.

3. Make the brownie batter according to the directions on the package. Place equal amounts of brownie batter into thirty of the prepared cupcake cavities, about 1 tablespoon each.

4. Place the pans in the preheated oven, and bake for 15 to 17 minutes. Remove the pan from the oven and place on a wire cooling rack. Let cool completely.

5. Place the buttercream frosting in the pastry bag and cut off a small hole at the tip. Squirt a small amount (about 1 tablespoon) of the buttercream in the center of each brownie (or spread the buttercream with a knife). Dip the brownie upside down in the plate of coconut, making sure plenty of it adheres to the frosting. Decorate by placing two to three colored jelly beans in the center of each nest.

Spring Garden Jenny Cookies

IF YOU WISH TO MAKE ALL THE SUGAR COOKIES ON THE SPRING GARDEN TABLE
AS THEY'RE PICTURED, YOU'LL NEED TWO BATCHES OF BUTTERCREAM FROSTING. THEN DIVIDE
AND TINT EACH WITH THE APPROPRIATE COLORS (PINK, PURPLE, ORANGE, YELLOW, PALE GREEN
AND BLUE). IT'LL SAVE YOU TIME IF YOU TINT THE BUTTERCREAM AND FILL EACH
PASTRY BAG BEFORE YOU BEGIN DECORATING.

ATTACH WILTON DECORATING TIPS AND COUPLERS TO EACH OF THE PASTRY BAGS AND FILL
WITH FROSTING INCLUDING ONE BAG OF WHITE BUTTERCREAM. THE COOKIES ON THIS TABLE
USE A NUMBER OF PASTRY BAGS—SEVEN IN ALL—SO IT'S BETTER IN THE LONG RUN TO USE
DISPOSABLE BAGS AND THROW THEM AWAY WHEN YOU'RE DONE. IF YOU DON'T HAVE
ENOUGH DECORATING TIPS FOR ALL THE BAGS, JUST CHANGE THEM OUT, WASH THEM,
AND PUT THEM IN ANOTHER BAG (USING COUPLERS MAKES CHANGING TIPS SO EASY).
YOU'LL BE MAKING TWO BATCHES OF SUGAR COOKIE DOUGH AND USING IT FOR ALL THE
COOKIE SHAPES, INCLUDING THE BUNNY EAR COOKIES FOR THE BUNNY EAR
CUPCAKES. SEE PAGE 12 IN THE "BASICS" CHAPTER FOR
SUGAR COOKIE INGREDIENTS AND DIRECTIONS.

MAKES 24 COOKIES

YOU WILL NEED

ROLLING PIN
2 NONSTICK COOKIE SHEETS
COOKIE SPATULA
ROUND COOKIE CUTTER
CARROT COOKIE CUTTER
BUNNY FACE COOKIE CUTTER
7 DISPOSABLE PASTRY BAGS
2 #4 WILTON DECORATING TIPS
1 #1M WILTON DECORATING TIP
1 #103 WILTON DECORATING TIP
6 WILTON COUPLERS
AMERICOLOR SOFT GEL PASTE
COLORS; PINK, PURPLE, ORANGE,
YELLOW, MINT GREEN AND SKY BLUE

Pink and Purple Flower Cookies

COOKIE INGREDIENTS

PINK BUTTERCREAM
PURPLE BUTTERCREAM

To decorate the pink and purple flower cookies, place the cookies on the cake turntable. Using the pastry bags filled with pink and purple frosting, and fitted with a #103 Wilton decorating tip, beginning with fat end of tip closer to cookie and skinny end pointing up, begin to squeeze icing bag while also spinning turntable to create ruffled flower petals. Spin and squeeze until entire circle is filled.

(continued)

Yellow Rose Cookies

INGREDIENTS

YELLOW BUTTERCREAM

To decorate the yellow rose cookies, use the pastry bag filled with yellow frosting and fitted with a #1M Wilton decorating tip. Starting from the center of the cookie, begin to squeeze decorating bag using consistent pressure, and in clockwise motion, swirl around, to create a rose.

Garden Carrot Cookies

INGREDIENTS

ORANGE BUTTERCREAM

PALE GREEN BUTTERCREAM

To decorate the carrot cookies, use the pastry bag filled with orange frosting and fitted with a #4 Wilton decorating tip. Outline the carrot with orange frosting avoiding the carrot greens on top. Fill in the outline with orange frosting, running it horizontally from one side to the other until it is completely filled in. Draw stems at the top of the carrot using the pastry bag filled with pale green frosting and #4 tip so it resembles carrot greens.

Bunny Ear Cookies

INGREDIENTS

WHITE BUTTERCREAM

PINK BUTTERCREAM

To decorate the Bunny Ear cookies, use the pastry bag filled with white frosting and fitted with a #4 Wilton decorating tip. Outline the entire cookie, ears and all, with frosting. Fill in the outline with white frosting, running it horizontally from one side to the other until it is completely filled in. Color the inside of the ears using the pastry bag with pink frosting and #4 tip.

6

Ice Cream Shop

A FEW YEARS AGO, A BRIDE AND GROOM ASKED ME TO CREATE A CUSTOM DESSERT TABLE FOR THEIR WEDDING. THE BRIDE MENTIONED THAT THEY LOVED TO GO OUT FOR ICE CREAM. AS SOON AS SHE SAID THAT, I IMMEDIATELY THOUGHT: ICE CREAM SHOP! GRANTED, IT WOULD BE A VERY UNIQUE TABLE FOR A WEDDING, BUT THEY LOVED THE IDEA. I'D CREATE ALL SORTS OF FUN ICE CREAM THEMED DESSERTS WHILE INCORPORATING THEIR WEDDING COLORS.

I HEADED TO THE GROCERY STORE AND DOWN THE FROZEN ICE CREAM AISLE FOR INSPIRATION (AND YOU SHOULD, TOO). I PICKED UP WAFFLE BOWLS AND CONES, MINIATURE CONES, NUT TOPPINGS AND RAINBOW SPRINKLES, AND WENT BACK TO MY KITCHEN TO GET CREATIVE.

You can use my core group of desserts and inspiration from your local market to do the same thing. Make sugar cookies using ice cream cone and ice cream sundae shapes. Bake brownies extra thin and sandwich them between icing to create ice cream sandwiches. And it's easy to shape Rice Krispie treats like ice cream bars and cake pops as miniature ice cream cones.

For a cake, try using a Rice Krispie treat base. Make three balls (or scoops) out of Rice Krispie treats, then cover each scoop with cake pop mixture. After refrigerating the scoops, dip each one into candy melts and stack them onto a vintage milk glass vase (easily found on ebay or etsy) to create a life-size ice cream cone. It's the perfect centerpiece.

SETTING THE TABLE

To create the ultimate ice cream shop dessert table, begin with a colorful backdrop and awning. It's easy to make by attaching bright pink fabric to a piece of plywood with a staple gun. I completed the look with a striped awning made by my favorite local seamstress that resembled an old fashioned ice cream parlor. A striped fabric bunting banner is equally adorable, strung from the backdrop. Since the desserts are so colorful and bright, simple white cake plates are the perfect display pieces. Line an old drawer with Styrofoam and use it to display cake pops covered in a bed of rainbow sprinkles. Then turn an old box or crate upside down to create height on your table, add a homemade Ice Cream sign to your backdrop. Before you know it, your guests will be screaming for ice cream.

ICE CREAM SHOP DESSERTS

♥ **Ice Cream Cone Cake**

♥ **Single Scoop of Vanilla Cupcakes**

♥ **Strawberry Sugar Cone Cake Pops**

♥ **Rice Krispie Treat Ice Cream Bars**

♥ **Brownie Waffle Bowl Sundaes**

♥ **Dilly Bars**

♥ **Mini Banana Split Bites**

♥ **Brownie Ice Cream Sandwiches**

♥ **Birthday Cake Waffle Cone Cake Pops**

♥ **Ice Cream Cone Cookies**

♥ **Ice Cream Sundae Cookies**

Ice Cream Cone Cake

PARTY GUESTS WILL GO CRAZY FOR THIS ICE CREAM CONE CAKE MADE FROM RICE KRISPIE TREATS, CAKE POP MIXTURE AND MELTED CANDY CHOCOLATES. CHANGE THE COLORS OF YOUR MELTED CANDY FOR DIFFERENT "FLAVORED" ICE CREAM SCOOPS.

Note: Five to six packages of candy melts? Yes, you read that right! This is a very large dessert. The melted candy has to be deep enough so you can dip the cake covered Rice Krispie balls and completely cover them. You'll more than likely end up with some extra melted candy at the bottom of the bowl, but not to worry. It can be remelted and used in another recipe in this book.

MAKES ONE TRIPLE SCOOP CAKE

INGREDIENTS

5 TABLESPOONS (70 G) BUTTER OR MARGARINE

1½ (10-OUNCE [280 G] PACKAGES) MINI MARSHMALLOWS (6 CUPS)

9 CUPS (225 G) RICE KRISPIES CEREAL

COOKING SPRAY OR CRISCO OR BUTTER PLUS FLOUR, FOR PANS

1 (18.25-OUNCE [517 G]) BOX DUNCAN HINES DEVIL'S FOOD CAKE MIX

1 (3.4-OUNCE [110 G]) BOX JELL-O CHOCOLATE INSTANT PUDDING AND PIE FILLING, DRY

1 CUP (235 ML) WATER

⅓ CUP (80 ML) OIL

4 LARGE EGGS

½ TO ¾ CUP (120 TO 175 ML) BUTTERCREAM FROSTING (PAGE 10), PLUS MORE FOR DECORATION

5 TO 6 (12-OUNCE [340 G]) PACKAGES WHITE CANDY MELTS

PINK CANDY OIL

RED GUMBALL

RAINBOW SPRINKLES

DIRECTIONS FOR THE RICE KRISPIE BARS:

1. In large saucepan over low heat, melt the butter. Add the marshmallows and stir until melted and smooth. Remove the pan from the heat.

2. Add the Rice Krispies and stir until completely coated. Let cool just enough to handle.

3. Divide and shape the Rice Krispie treat mixture into three balls (small, medium and large) and let harden.

DIRECTIONS FOR THE CAKE POP MIXTURE:

1. Preheat the oven to 350°F (180°C). Coat the 9 × 13-inch (23 × 33 cm) baking pan with cooking spray, or grease and flour the pan, tapping out the excess flour. Set aside.

2. In a large bowl, and using an electric stand mixer fitted with a paddle attachment, beat the cake mix, pudding mix, water, oil and eggs on medium speed for 2 to 3 minutes, or until well blended. Scrape the sides of the bowl and mix again until all the ingredients are incorporated.

3. Pour the batter into the prepared pan. Place the pan in the preheated oven, and bake for 35 to 40 minutes, or until a toothpick inserted into the center comes out clean.

4. Remove the pan from the oven and place on a wire cooling rack for 25 to 30 minutes. Let cool completely before making the ice cream cone cake.

5. Mash up the cake and place in a large bowl. Using an electric stand mixer fitted with a paddle attachment, mix the cake and ½ to ¾ cup (120 to 175 ml) of frosting on medium speed until well blended and the mixture can be molded into a ball.

6. With your hands, cover each Rice Krispie ball with the cake ball mixture, packing it on tightly until they are completely covered and feel firm. Set aside on a cookie sheet.

7. Refrigerate for 1 hour.

(continued)

9 × 13-INCH (23 × 33 CM) BAKING PAN
OR CASSEROLE DISH

LARGE MILK GLASS VASE, OR OTHER
SUITABLE VASE LARGE ENOUGH TO
HOLD ICE CREAM CONE CAKE

1 (¼-INCH [6 MM]-DIAMETER) LONG
WOODEN DOWEL, ABOUT 12 INCHES
(30.5 CM) LONG

3 (6- TO 9-INCH [15 TO 23 CM]-LONG)
DOWELS

PASTRY BAG

#1M WILTON DECORATING TIP

DIRECTIONS FOR ASSEMBLING THE ICE CREAM CONE CAKE:

1. Melt the five to six packages of candy melts in a deep microwave-safe bowl in 30-second increments at 40% power for about 3 to 4 minutes, stirring as needed until smooth. Stick a smaller dowel into each of the cake coated Rice Krispie balls. Dip the largest ball into the white melted candy and place it on the widest opening of the milk glass vase while still wet. Carefully remove the dowel.

2. Add enough pink candy oil to the remaining melted white candy and stir until a light pink color is achieved. Dip the medium-size ball into the melted candy and stack it on top of the large ball, pressing down lightly to adhere. Remove the dowel.

3. Add a few more drops of pink candy oil to the remaining melted candy and stir to create a bright pink color. Dip the smallest ball into the candy and stack that on top of the two other balls. Remove the dowel.

4. Force the long dowel all the way down through the center of all the balls to keep the cone stable. Let dry.

5. Place the #1M Wilton decorating tip inside the pastry bag (no need to use a coupler) and fill with the buttercream frosting. Decorate the top of the ice cream cone to resemble whipped cream and to cover the hole where the dowel was placed. Sprinkle rainbow sprinkles on whipped cream. Place a red cherry gumball on top.

Single Scoop of Vanilla Cupcakes

THESE VANILLA CUPCAKES ARE TWO DELICIOUS DESSERTS IN ONE. HERE, YOU GET THE FLAVOR OF A RICH VANILLA CAKE BUT ALSO THE BUTTERY CRUNCH OF A MINIATURE JENNY COOKIE TOPPER. MINI SUGAR COOKIES MAKE GREAT TOPPERS WHEN YOU WANT TO ADD A BIT MORE DECOR TO YOUR CUPCAKES.

MAKES 24 STANDARD-SIZE CUPCAKES

INGREDIENTS

1 (18.25-OUNCE [517 G]) BOX DUNCAN HINES FRENCH VANILLA CAKE MIX

1 (3.4-OUNCE [110 G]) BOX JELL-O FRENCH VANILLA INSTANT PUDDING AND PIE FILLING, DRY

1 CUP (235 ML) WATER

⅓ CUP (80 ML) OIL

4 LARGE EGGS

1 BATCH BUTTERCREAM FROSTING (PAGE 10)

MINI ICE CREAM CONE SUGAR COOKIES FOR DECORATION

YOU WILL NEED

2 CUPCAKE TRAYS

24 MINI PAPER CUPCAKE LINERS

SMALL COOKIE SCOOP

DIRECTIONS

1. Preheat the oven to 350°F (180°C). Line the mini cupcake trays with twenty-four paper cupcake liners. Set the trays aside.

2. In a large bowl, and using an electric stand mixer fitted with a paddle attachment, beat the cake mix, pudding mix, water, oil and eggs on medium speed for 2 to 3 minutes, or until well blended. Scrape down the sides of the bowl, and mix again until all the ingredients are incorporated.

3. Using a cookie scoop, place one scoop of cake batter (filling about two-thirds full) in each paper liner, dividing evenly between the cupcake trays to create a perfectly even batch of cupcakes.

4. Bake the cupcakes for 18 to 20 minutes, or until a toothpick inserted into the center comes out clean. Remove the cupcakes from the oven and place the trays on the wire cooling racks for 5 minutes.

5. Meanwhile, make one batch of buttercream icing.

6. Take the cupcakes out of the trays and allow them to cool completely on the wire racks before decorating.

7. To decorate, using a cookie scoop, plop the buttercream frosting on top so that it resembles a scoop of vanilla ice cream. Decorate each cupcake with one mini ice cream cone sugar cookie.

Strawberry Sugar Cone Cake Pops

EVERYTHING IS CUTER WHEN IT'S MINI. NOT A STRAWBERRY FAN? SWAP THIS CAKE RECIPE FOR YOUR FAVORITE CAKE POP FLAVOR.

MAKES 40 CAKE POPS

INGREDIENTS

COOKING SPRAY OR CRISCO OR BUTTER PLUS FLOUR, FOR PAN

1 (18.25-OUNCE [517 G]) BOX DUNCAN HINES STRAWBERRY CAKE MIX

1 (3.4-OUNCE [110 G]) BOX JELL-O VANILLA INSTANT PUDDING AND PIE FILLING, DRY

1 CUP (235 ML) WATER

⅓ CUP (80 ML) OIL

4 LARGE EGGS

½ TO ¾ CUP (120 TO 175 ML) BUTTERCREAM FROSTING (PAGE 10)

1 (42-CUP) BOX JOY BRAND MINI SUGAR CONES

3 (12-OUNCE [340 G]) PACKAGE WHITE CANDY MELTS

40 PINK SIXLETS

RAINBOW JIMMIES

YOU WILL NEED

9 × 13-INCH (23 × 33 CM) BAKING PAN OR CASSEROLE DISH

DIRECTIONS

1. Preheat the oven to 350°F (180°C). Coat the 9 × 13-inch (23 × 33 cm) baking pan with cooking spray, or grease and flour the pan, tapping out the excess flour. Set aside.

2. In a large bowl, and using an electric stand mixer fitted with a paddle attachment, beat the cake mix, pudding mix, water, oil and eggs on medium speed for 2 to 3 minutes, or until well blended. Scrape the sides of the bowl and mix again until all the ingredients are incorporated.

3. Pour the batter into the prepared cake pan. Place the pan in the preheated oven, and bake for 35 to 40 minutes, or until a toothpick inserted into the center comes out clean.

4. Remove the pan from the oven and place on a wire cooling rack for 25 to 30 minutes. Let cool completely before making the cake pops.

5. Mash up the cake and place in a large bowl. Using an electric stand mixer fitted with a paddle attachment, mix the cake and ½ to ¾ cup (120 to 275 ml) of frosting on medium speed until well blended and the mixture can be molded into a ball. Measure and roll the mixture into tablespoon-size balls. Refrigerate for 1 hour, or until firm.

6. Melt the candy melts in a microwave-safe bowl in 30-second increments at 40% power for about 2½ minutes, stirring as needed until smooth.

7. Barely dip the top of the Mini Cup cones into the melted candy, just enough to put a ring around the top of the cone. Place cone upside down on top of the refrigerated cake balls. This helps the candy adhere to the cake balls. Continue until all are finished.

8. Dip the cake balls (with the cone attached) into the melted candy, completely coating it to the edge of the cone. Sprinkle with rainbow jimmies and top each with a pink Sixlet candy while the melted candy is still wet.

Rice Krispie Treat Ice Cream Bars

KIDS LOVE THESE FUN RICE KRISPIE ICE CREAM BARS. THEY'RE FUN TO MAKE AND EASY TO EAT WITH THE POPSICLE STICK HANDLE. PARENTS WILL LOVE THAT THESE ICE CREAM BARS DON'T MELT INTO A STICKY MESS.

MAKES 9 ICE CREAM BARS

INGREDIENTS

VEGETABLE SPRAY

5 TABLESPOONS (70 G) BUTTER OR MARGARINE

1½ (10-OUNCE [280 G] PACKAGES) MINI MARSHMALLOWS (6 CUPS)

9 CUPS (250 G) RICE KRISPIES CEREAL

1 (12-OUNCE [340 G)]) PACKAGE WHITE CANDY MELTS

PINK CANDY OIL

RAINBOW SPRINKLES

YOU WILL NEED

WILTON ICE CREAM BAR PAN, OR 9 × 13-INCH (13 × 33 CM) BAKING PAN OR CASSEROLE DISH

ROUND COOKIE CUTTER

9 OVERSIZE POPSICLE CRAFT STICKS

STYROFOAM

DIRECTIONS

1. Lightly oil or spray a Wilton ice cream bar pan, or the 9 × 13-inch (23 × 33 cm) baking pan with vegetable spray.

2. In a large saucepan over low heat, melt the butter. Add the marshmallows and stir until melted and smooth. Remove the pan from the heat.

3. Add the Rice Krispies and stir until completely coated. Pat into the prepared baking pan and let cool completely to set.

4. If using the 9 × 13-inch (23 × 33 cm) pan, cut into nine rectangle shapes. Remove the bars from the pan and insert a Popsicle stick into each end. Using a round cookie cutter, round off the tops, then use cutter upside down and cut a "bite" out of the ice cream bar.

5. In a small microwave-safe bowl, melt the entire package of candy melts in the microwave at 30-second increments at 40% power. Continue for about 1½ minutes, or until all they are thoroughly melted, stirring every 30 seconds. Add the pink candy and stir again.

6. Dip the bars in the melted candy and sprinkle with rainbow sprinkles. The messier and drippier the better! I let my ice cream bars dry in a block of Styrofoam rather than laying them on waxed paper.

Brownie Waffle Bowl Sundaes

THIS CHOCOLATY CANDY-COATED BROWNIE IS DISGUISED AS AN ICE CREAM SUNDAE. SUBSTITUTE SPRINKLES FOR CHOPPED NUTS, OR SWAP THE MINI SNICKERS CANDY WITH A REESE'S PEANUT BUTTER CUP FOR A FUN CHANGE OF FLAVOR.

MAKES 10 BROWNIE SUNDAES

INGREDIENTS

1 STANDARD PACKAGE DUNCAN HINES BROWNIE MIX, PLUS ADDITIONAL BOX INGREDIENTS

1 (7-OUNCE [196 G]) PACKAGE MINI SNICKERS BARS

1 PACKAGE WAFFLE BOWLS

1 CUP WHITE CANDY MELTS

RAINBOW SPRINKLES

RED GUMBALLS

YOU WILL NEED

NONSTICK CUPCAKE TRAY

WOODEN CRAFT SPOONS (FOUND AT MOST CRAFT SHOPS)

DIRECTIONS

1. Preheat the oven to 350°F (180°C). Lightly oil or spray the cupcake tray with vegetable spray.

2. Make the brownie batter according to the directions on the package.

3. Scoop 1 tablespoon of brownie batter into the greased cupcake tray. Place one mini Snickers bar into the batter, and top with additional tablespoon of brownie batter.

4. Bake for 15 to 18 minutes, or until a toothpick inserted into the top comes out clean.

5. Remove the tray from the oven and place on a wire cooling rack. Let cool completely before making waffle sundaes.

6. When cool, place a brownie into each waffle bowl

7. Melt 1 cup of candy melts in a microwave-safe bowl in 30-second increments at 40% power for about 1½ minutes, stirring as needed until smooth. Pour the melted candy in the pastry bag and cut off the tip.

8. Top the brownies with the melted candy, letting it drizzle over the brownies. Top with rainbow sprinkles and a red cherry gumball while the candy is still wet. Insert a wooden craft spoon.

Dilly Bars

BE SURE TO MAKE PLENTY OF THESE DELICIOUS PEANUT BUTTER CRACKER COOKIES CAMOUFLAGED AS CLASSIC CHOCOLATE-COVERED ICE CREAM DILLY BARS. THEY'LL FLY OFF YOUR DESSERT TABLE ONCE KIDS FIND OUT WHAT'S INSIDE.

MAKES 18 TREATS

INGREDIENTS

1 PACKAGE (SLEEVE OF 36) RITZ CRACKERS

1 CUP (260 G) SMOOTH PEANUT BUTTER (I USE JIF)

2 (12-OUNCE [340 G]) PACKAGES MILK CHOCOLATE CANDY MELTS

1½ CUPS (225 G) CHOPPED WALNUTS

YOU WILL NEED

DISPOSABLE PASTRY BAG

18 POPSICLE STICKS

KITCHEN FORK

STYROFOAM

DIRECTIONS

1. 1. Turn the Ritz crackers upside down on a cookie sheet.

2. Fill the pastry bag with peanut butter and cut the tip. Pipe a dollop of peanut butter on half of the crackers. Place the remaining crackers on top to make sandwiches.

3. Insert a Popsicle stick into each sandwich.

4. Melt the chocolate candy melts in a microwave-safe bowl in 30-second increments at 40% power for about 2½ minutes, stirring as needed until smooth.

5. Dip the crackers into the melted chocolate, and sprinkle with the chopped nuts.

6. Stand the Dilly Bars in a sheet of Styrofoam to dry.

Mini Banana Split Bites

KIDS ADORE THESE FUN AND (SOMEWHAT) HEALTHY TREATS. MAKE A BATCH OF THESE
FOR A FUN BRING-TO-PRESCHOOL TREAT OR A PLAY-DATE SNACK.

MAKES 12 BANANA SPLITS

INGREDIENTS

4 RIPE BANANAS

**1 (12-OUNCE [340 G]) PACKAGE MILK
CHOCOLATE CANDY MELTS**

RAINBOW SPRINKLES

**1 CUP (235 ML) BUTTERCREAM
FROSTING (PAGE 10)**

12 RED GUMBALLS

YOU WILL NEED

WAXED PAPER

DISPOSABLE PASTRY BAG

#1M WILTON DECORATING TIP

DIRECTIONS

1. Melt the chocolate candy melts in a microwave-safe bowl in 30-second increments at 40% power for about 1½ minutes, stirring as needed until smooth.

2. Peel and cut off the ends of the bananas and discard. Cut each banana into three pieces. Dip the ends into melted chocolate candy and sprinkle with the rainbow sprinkles. Place upright on waxed paper to dry.

3. Place the #1M Wilton decorating tip inside the pastry bag (no need to use a coupler) and fill with the buttercream frosting. Decorate the top of the banana splits to resemble whipped cream. Place a red cherry gumball on top.

Brownie
Ice Cream Sandwiches

SIMPLE BROWNIES BECOME GOURMET WITH JUST A SPOONFUL OF MY FAMOUS BUTTERCREAM FROSTING SANDWICHED IN BETWEEN. DIP IN SPRINKLES OF ANY COLOR TO COORDINATE ANY PARTY THEME.

MAKES 12 ICE CREAM SANDWICHES

INGREDIENTS

VEGETABLE SPRAY

1 STANDARD BOX DUNCAN HINES BROWNIE MIX PLUS ADDITIONAL INGREDIENTS ON BOX

2 CUPS (475 ML) BUTTERCREAM FROSTING (PAGE 10)

1 LARGE JAR RAINBOW SPRINKLES (ABOUT 1 CUP)

YOU WILL NEED

JELLY-ROLL PAN

DISPOSABLE PASTRY BAG

DIRECTIONS

1. Preheat the oven to 350°F (180°C). Lightly oil or the spray jelly-roll pan with vegetable spray.

2. Make the brownie batter according to the directions on the package. Spread the batter in the prepared pan and bake for 15 to 18 minutes, or until a toothpick comes out clean. Remove the pan from the oven and place on a wire cooling rack. Let cool completely.

3. Cut the brownies into 24 rectangular pieces.

4. Fill the pastry bag with the buttercream frosting. Cut off the tip of the bag and pipe the frosting on half the brownies. Place the remaining brownies on top to resemble sandwiches.

5. Place the rainbow sprinkles on a plate. Dip the sides of each brownie sandwich into the sprinkles so that they stick to the frosting.

Birthday Cake
Waffle Cone Cake Pops

CAKE POP QUEEN BAKERELLA—WHO ORIGINATED THE CAKE POP PHENOMENON—FIRST MADE THESE ADORABLE WAFFLE CONE CAKE POPS BACK IN 2010. WITH A SWAP OF CAKE FLAVOR AND CHANGE OF CANDY COLOR, I'VE PUT MY OWN TWIST ON THESE DELIGHTFUL LITTLE TREATS. STAND THEM UPRIGHT IN A BED OF COLORFUL SPRINKLES AND DISPLAY THEM PROUDLY ON YOUR TABLE.

MAKES 40 CAKE POPS

INGREDIENTS

COOKING SPRAY OR CRISCO OR BUTTER PLUS FLOUR, FOR PAN

1 (18.25-OUNCE [517 G]) BOX DUNCAN HINES FUNFETTI CAKE MIX

1 (3.4-OUNCE [110 G]) BOX JELL-O VANILLA INSTANT PUDDING AND PIE FILLING, DRY

1 CUP (235 ML) WATER

⅓ CUP (80 ML) OIL

4 LARGE EGGS

1 PACKAGE BIRTHDAY CAKE OREOS, CRUSHED

½ TO ¾ CUP (120 TO 175 ML) BUTTERCREAM FROSTING (PAGE 10)

40 WAFFLE CONES

3 (12-OUNCE [340 G]) PACKAGES WHITE CANDY MELTS

40 PINK SIXLETS

PINK CANDY OIL

YOU WILL NEED

9 × 13-INCH (23 × 33 CM) BAKING PAN OR CASSEROLE DISH

SERRATED KNIFE

STYROFOAM

DISPOSABLE PASTRY BAG

DIRECTIONS

1. Preheat the oven to 350°F (180°C). Coat the 9 × 13-inch (23 × 33 cm) baking pan with cooking spray, or grease and flour the pan, tapping out the excess flour. Set aside.

2. In a large bowl, and using an electric stand mixer fitted with a paddle attachment, beat the cake mix, pudding mix, water, oil and eggs on medium speed for 2 to 3 minutes, or until well blended. Scrape the sides of the bowl and mix again until all the ingredients are incorporated.

3. Pour the batter into the prepared cake pan. Place the pan in the preheated oven, and bake for 35 to 40 minutes, or until a toothpick inserted into the center comes out clean.

4. Remove the pan from the oven and place on a wire cooling rack for 25 to 30 minutes. Let cool completely before making the cake pops.

5. Mash up the cake and place in a large bowl. Using an electric stand mixer fitted with a paddle attachment, mix the cake, crushed Oreos and ½ to ¾ cup (120 to 175 ml) of frosting on medium speed until well blended and the mixture can be molded into a ball.

6. Measure and roll the mixture into tablespoon-size balls, place on a cookie sheet and refrigerate for 1 hour, or until firm.

7. Using a serrated knife, carefully saw off the top third of each waffle cone to make their size in scale to a cake pop.

8. Melt the candy melts in a microwave-safe bowl in 30-second increments at 40% power for about 2 to 3 minutes, stirring as needed until smooth. Remove the bowl from the microwave. Add the pink candy oil and stir again.

9. Barely dip the top of the waffle cone into the melted candy, just enough to put a ring around the top of the cone. Place the cone upside down on top of the refrigerated cake balls. This helps the candy adhere to the cake balls. Continue until all are finished.

10. Dip the cake balls (with waffle cone attached) into the melted candy, completely coating them to the edge of the cone. Stand the cones upright in Styrofoam to dry.

11. Once all the cones are dipped, add the pink candy oil to the remaining melted white candy. Fill the disposable pastry bag with the melted candy, cut the tip cut off and drizzle over each cake pop. The messier the better! Top each with a pink Sixlet candy while the candy is still wet. Return the cake pops to the Styrofoam to finish drying.

Ice Cream Shop Jenny Cookies

THESE COLORFUL SUGAR COOKIES ARE ALWAYS A HIT AT MY PARTIES. USING WILTON'S #18 TIP, THEY'RE EASILY DECORATED TO RESEMBLE REAL ICE CREAM.

YOU'LL ONLY USE TWO REGULAR-SIZE COOKIE CUTTERS FOR THE ICE CREAM CONE COOKIES AND THE ICE CREAM SUNDAE COOKIES, LEAVING YOU PLENTY OF EXTRA DOUGH TO MAKE THE CUTEST AND TEENIEST MINI ICE CREAM CONE COOKIES FOR DECORATIONS ON TOP OF THE SINGLE SCOOP OF VANILLA CUPCAKES. THESE COOKIES REQUIRE LIGHT PINK, DARK PINK, BROWN AND WHITE FROSTING, SO YOU'LL NEED ONE BATCH OF BUTTERCREAM FROSTING (PAGE 10). DECORATE THE COOKIES WITH THE WHITE FROSTING FIRST (YOU'LL USE MORE WHITE FROSTING THAN THE OTHER COLORS), THEN TINT THE REMAINING FROSTING WITH THE COLORS NEEDED; LIGHT PINK, DARK PINK AND BROWN. ATTACH WILTON DECORATING TIPS AND COUPLERS TO EACH OF THE PASTRY BAGS AND FILL WITH FROSTING. FOLLOW THE DIRECTIONS FOR EACH COOKIE AS DESCRIBED BELOW. SEE PAGE 12 FOR THE COOKIE INGREDIENTS AND DIRECTIONS.

MAKES ABOUT 24 COOKIES

YOU WILL NEED

ROLLING PIN

2 NONSTICK COOKIE SHEETS

COOKIE SPATULA

ICE CREAM CONE COOKIE CUTTER

ICE CREAM SUNDAE COOKIE CUTTER

MINI ICE CREAM CONE COOKIE CUTTER (THE SMALLEST YOU CAN FIND)

4 DISPOSABLE PASTRY BAGS

4 #4 WILTON DECORATING TIPS

4 #18 WILTON DECORATING TIPS

4 WILTON COUPLERS

AMERICOLOR SOFT GEL PASTE COLORS TO MAKE LIGHT PINK, DARK PINK AND BROWN

PINK SIXLETS CANDIES

RAINBOW SPRINKLES

Ice Cream Cone Cookies

INGREDIENTS

WHITE BUTTERCREAM

BROWN BUTTERCREAM

DARK PINK BUTTERCREAM

LIGHT PINK BUTTERCREAM

PINK SPRINKLES

PINK SIXLETS CANDIES

To decorate the ice cream cone cookies, place dark pink, white and brown buttercream frosting in separate pastry bags each fitted with a #4 Wilton decorating tip. Begin by outlining the bottom half of the cone with brown frosting. Beginning at the bottom tip, fill in the outline with brown frosting, running it horizontally from one edge of the outline to the other, until the bottom of the cone is filled in. Make crisscross marks diagonally across the cone to resemble a waffle cone. Using your pink icing with #18 tip and a swirly motion, add a fluffy layer/row of pink ice cream to the top of the cone tip. With your white icing with #18 tip, outline the top scoop of ice cream. Fill in using swirly motion. Sprinkle top of cookies with pink sprinkles, and decorate with a pink Sixlet candy on top for the cherry.

Ice Cream Sundae Cookies

INGREDIENTS
WHITE BUTTERCREAM
PINK BUTTERCREAM
PALE PINK BUTTERCREAM

These ice cream sugar cookies are just as delicious as they are adorable. Sweet swirled buttercream resembling drippy ice cream is easy to achieve with Wilton tip #18.

To decorate the ice cream sundae cookies, place light pink, dark pink and brown buttercream frosting in separate pastry bags each fitted with a #18 Wilton decorating tip. Use a #4 Wilton decorating tip for the white buttercream. Begin by outlining the sundae dish with white icing (#4 tip). Use pale pink icing with #18 tip and with a swirled hand motion, create a fluffy layer of pale pink ice cream. Repeat with brown icing to create a layer of chocolate ice cream. Top with white icing to create top layer of vanilla ice cream. Finish off the ice cream sundae cookie with a dot of pink icing (#18 tip) to resemble a cherry.

Mini Ice Cream Cone Cookies

FOR SINGLE SCOOP OF VANILLA CUPCAKES DECORATION

To decorate the mini ice cream cone cookies, using all four colors already in the pastry bags each fitted with #4 decorating tips, begin by outlining the bottom of the cones with brown frosting. Fill in the outline with more brown frosting. These are very teeny cookies, so do the best you can to make a cone. Decorate the remaining cookie with a small dollop of light pink, then white frosting on top resembling mini scoops of ice cream. Finish with one dot of with dark pink frosting to resemble the cherry on top.

7

Down on the Farm

IN LATE 2012, MY HUSBAND DAN AND I PURCHASED A 1937 FARMHOUSE IN LAKE STEVENS, WASHINGTON. WE'D BEEN LOOKING FOR A COUPLE OF YEARS AND HAD ZERO LUCK. WE WANTED ACREAGE, CHARACTER—AND I WANTED A WRAPAROUND PORCH. IN EARLY DECEMBER, MY HUSBAND TEXTED ME "911." AS A MOM, YOU GO TO THE UGLY PLACE: WHAT HAPPENED TO MY KIDS? IS EVERYONE OK? ALIVE? HOUSE ON FIRE?

EVERYONE WAS FINE. BUT A HOUSE HAD JUST BEEN PUT ON THE MARKET, AND HE WANTED TO BE THE FIRST TO SEE IT. AT 9 O'CLOCK THE NEXT MORNING, WE MET OUR REALTOR TO CHECK OUT THE FARM. I WAS UNSURE. IT HAD ZERO CURB APPEAL. BUT DAN CONVINCED ME OTHERWISE: WE COULD BUILD A PORCH, RIP OUT WALLS, AND ADD ON. "AND YOU CAN HAVE THE KITCHEN OF YOUR DREAMS!" HE SAID. NOW, AFTER PLENTY OF WORK, WE DO HAVE OUR DREAM HOME. THE KELLER FARMHOUSE HAS AN INCREDIBLE WRAPAROUND PORCH WITH FIVE ACRES OF GORGEOUS MOUNTAIN VIEWS, TREES, A POND, THREE ADORABLE GOATS, TWO CATS, ONE DUCK AND MORE ON THE WAY. AND I HAVE A TERRIFIC KITCHEN.

The farmhouse dream must have buried itself in my subconscious and emerged when it was time to throw Hudson his third birthday party. I'd found little felt barns in the dollar section at Target. They were a bit random, but I knew they'd make the perfect party-favor packaging. I couldn't pass them up so I tossed twenty into my cart (yes, I'm a bit of a hoarder), and decided Hudson would have a farm birthday party.

I scoured antique stores for anything farm related. I found colorful tin trays, an old wooden toy barn, wood crates and lots of vintage fabrics. I sent invitations in burlap bags with scraps of hay sticking out, tied in red bandanas. I won't reveal the shipping cost, but I convinced myself that Hudson only turned three once and justified the price. I baked miniature cherry pies with lattice crust, strawberry shortcakes in small canning jars and chocolate pigs sitting on a pile of muddy haystack treats. To this day, it is still my favorite party I've thrown.

SETTING THE TABLE

The table should be multicolored and include a variety of patterns. Red, blue, yellow, green and brown made up my color palette. With such a mixture of colors, it's easy to find fun props and display pieces. Lay a couple pieces of the floral fabrics across an old wood table as your tablecloth.

Try to create height and different levels with wooden crates and boxes. Turn an apple basket upside down and place a vintage wooden toy barn on top. My chocolate haystack Pigs in Mud treats can sit happily inside. Drape a few vintage fabrics over the crates and place desserts on yellow hobnail glass cake plates. Decorate white cake pops like cows, then display them in bales of hay. Place sugar cookies on vintage patterned trays.

My friend Scout (one of Tori Spelling's "Guncles") sent me an old-fashioned yellow tin cake box as a housewarming gift when we finished our farmhouse. While scouring my attic for farm party props, I saw the yellow box. It had to be included in the table. The color was perfect. I used it as my cake stand. This is the perfect example of using odd items for your displays.

I'd originally planned on using an old toy tractor as a cake topper, but as I was decorating it, I noticed the pile of vintage fabrics I'd picked up to use on the table. I grabbed my scissors and tore off a few strips of fabric. I tied them to wood dowels and stuck them into my cake. It was adorable. I loved the idea so much that I made smaller versions and used them for cupcake toppers, too. Don't be afraid to improvise!

Down on the Farm
DESSERTS

- ♥ **Farm Fresh Lemon Cupcakes**
- ♥ **Red Velvet Ribbon Cake**
- ♥ **Cookies and Cream Cow Cake Pops**
- ♥ **Strawberry Shortcakes in a Jar**
- ♥ **Pigs in Mud**
- ♥ **Lattice Crust Mini Cherry Pies**
- ♥ **Horse Cookies**
- ♥ **Cow Cookies**
- ♥ **Rooster Cookies**
- ♥ **Tractor Cookies**
- ♥ **Barn Cookies**
- ♥ **Sheep Cookies**
- ♥ **Pig Cookies**

Farm Fresh Lemon Cupcakes

THESE CUPCAKES GIVE MY DELICIOUS BUTTERCREAM A ZESTY LEMON TWIST. SWITCH UP YOUR DECORATING TECHNIQUES BY SWAPPING YOUR DECORATING TIP TO CREATE A DIFFERENT LOOK FOR YOUR CUPCAKE. TOPPERS ARE MADE WITH WOOD STICKS AND FABRIC SCRAPS.

MAKES 24 STANDARD CUPCAKES

INGREDIENTS

1 (18.25-OUNCE [517 G]) BOX DUNCAN HINES LEMON CAKE MIX

1 (3.4-OUNCE [110 G]) BOX JELL-O LEMON INSTANT PUDDING AND PIE FILLING, DRY

1 CUP (235 ML) WATER

⅓ CUP (80 ML) OIL

4 LARGE EGGS

2 TEASPOONS PURE LEMON EXTRACT

1 BATCH BUTTERCREAM FROSTING (PAGE 10)

AMERICOLOR YELLOW SOFT GEL PASTE COLOR

YOU WILL NEED

2 STANDARD-SIZE CUPCAKE TRAYS

24 STANDARD PAPER CUPCAKE LINERS

COOKIE SCOOP

1 LARGE PASTRY BAG

#1M WILTON DECORATING TIP

24 WOODEN CRAFT STICKS TIED WITH COLORED FABRIC SCRAP "FLAGS"

DIRECTIONS

1. Preheat the oven to 350°F (180°C). Line the cupcake trays with paper cupcake liners. Set the prepared pans aside.

2. In a large bowl, and using an electric stand mixer fitted with a paddle attachment, beat the cake mix, pudding mix, water, oil, eggs and 1 teaspoon of the lemon extract on medium speed for 2 to 3 minutes, or until well blended. Scrape down the sides of the bowl, and mix again until all the ingredients are incorporated.

3. Using a cookie scoop, fill each paper liner with batter about two-thirds full, dividing evenly between the cupcake trays.

4. Bake the cupcakes for 18 to 20 minutes, or until a toothpick inserted into the center comes out clean or tops spring back when lightly touched. Remove the cupcakes from the oven and place the trays on wire cooling racks for 15 minutes. Take the cupcakes out of the trays and allow them to cool completely on the wire racks before decorating.

5. Meanwhile, make the one batch of buttercream frosting.

6. Be sure to add the remaining teaspoon of the lemon extract to the frosting. Add yellow food coloring to the frosting until it reaches the desired shade. Place the #1M Wilton decorating tip inside the pastry bag (no need to use a coupler) and fill with frosting.

7. To decorate the cupcakes, hold the pastry bag in an upright position, starting from the outside circle. Squeeze the bag while going clockwise, to make a large swirly rosette, building each layer onto the next until you reach the top. Push one decorated wooden craft stick into the center of each cupcake.

Red Velvet Ribbon Cake

A TIERED CAKE SITTING PRETTY AT THE TOP OF THE TABLE LENDS AN IMPORTANT VERTICAL DESIGN ELEMENT. ADD THE VINTAGE FABRIC FLAGS TO THE TOP AND YOUR CAKE NOW HAS A PERSONALITY OF ITS OWN.

MAKES ONE 6-INCH (15 CM) AND 8-INCH (20.5 CM) TIERED CAKE

INGREDIENTS

COOKING SPRAY OR CRISCO OR BUTTER PLUS FLOUR, FOR PANS

2 (18.25-OUNCE [517 G]) BOXES DUNCAN HINES RED VELVET CAKE MIX

2 (3.4-OUNCE [110 G]) BOXES JELL-O CHOCOLATE INSTANT PUDDING AND PIE FILLING, DRY

2 CUPS (470 ML) WATER

⅔ CUP (157 ML) OIL

8 LARGE EGGS

3 BATCHES BUTTERCREAM FROSTING (PAGE 10)

AMERICOLOR RED SOFT GEL PASTE COLOR

YOU WILL NEED

2 (8 × 2-INCH [20.5 × 5 CM]) AND 2 (6 × 2-INCH [15 × 5 CM]) ROUND NONSTICK CAKE PANS

CAKE CUTTER OR LONG, SERRATED KNIFE

2 ROUND CARDBOARD OR PLASTIC CAKE BOARDS

OFFSET ANGLED SPATULA

LARGE PASTRY BAG

#104 WILTON DECORATING TIP

WILTON COUPLER

5 (¼-INCH [6 MM]-THICK) DOWELS OR THICK PLASTIC STRAWS

LARGE, FLAT SPATULA

CAKE DECORATING TURNTABLE

LARGE DECORATING SPATULA

DIRECTIONS FOR THE CAKE:

1. Preheat the oven to 350°F (180°C). Coat the 8-inch (20.5 cm) and 6-inch (15 cm) round nonstick cake pans with cooking spray, or grease and flour the pans, tapping out the excess flour. Set the prepared pans aside.

2. In a large bowl, and using an electric stand mixer fitted with a paddle attachment, beat the cake mix, pudding mix, water, oil and eggs on medium speed for 2 to 3 minutes, or until well blended. Scrape the sides of the bowl and mix again until all the ingredients are incorporated.

3. Pour the batter into the prepared cake pans, filling each one approximately three-quarters full.

4. Place the pans in the preheated oven, on the middle rack. Bake 6-inch (15 cm) cakes for 25 to 30 minutes, and 8-inch (20.5 cm) cakes for 30 to 35 minutes, or until a toothpick inserted into the center comes out clean.

5. Remove the pans from the oven and place on wire cooling racks for 25 to 30 minutes. Run a knife around the edges of the cakes, flip the pans over, and gently extract the cakes. Return the cakes to the wire racks and finish cooling completely before frosting and decorating. After the layers are cooled, freeze or refrigerate the cakes for 1 hour before decorating to reduce crumbs and make for a smoother icing process.

6. Meanwhile, make the three batches of buttercream frosting. Add red food coloring to the frosting until it reaches the desired shade. Tip: This cake is decorated with heavy icing. If you live in a warm climate, you may want to cut down the added milk, to thicken your frosting a bit.

TO ASSEMBLE AND DECORATE THE CAKE

1. Before decorating, trim the crowns from the cake tops with a cake cutter or long, serrated knife so they are flat and even.

2. Place one of the 8-inch (20.5 cm) cakes on a cake board cut side up. Using the angled cake spatula, spread about ½ cup (120 ml) of the buttercream frosting evenly across the top of the cake layer. Place the second 8-inch (20.5 cm) cakes on top of the first, with cut sides on the bottom, and spreading the buttercream frosting between each layer. Use the angled cake spatula to cover the cake completely with a very thin layer of icing (or crumb coat) to help reduce the amount of crumbs in the final coat of icing. Set the two-tiered 8-inch (20.5 cm) cake aside.

3. Repeat this process with the 6-inch (15 cm) cake layers, using another ½ cup (120 ml) of buttercream frosting between the layers, and icing the sides and top of the cake. Once the same process has been completed on the 6-inch (15 cm) cake layers, allow them to dry for 1 hour, or until the icing crusts.

4. Attach Wilton decorating tip #104, and the coupler to the pastry bag and fill with red frosting. Set aside.

5. Create supports for the smaller cake to sit atop the larger cake by placing the dowels into the top of the 8-inch (20.5 cm) cake. Insert the first dowel into the cake and use a pen to mark the dowel at the point where it just comes to the top of the cake. Remove the dowel and cut it at that mark. Cut three to four additional dowels or straws to the same length and place them in a circle, approximately 2 inches (5 cm) from the center of the cake, and evenly spaced. Using a large, flat spatula, carefully center and place the 6-inch (15 cm) tier on top of the 8-inch (20.5 cm) cake tier.

6. Place the cake on a rotating cake turntable. Using a large decorating spatula, frost the top of the cake smooth. Using the pastry bag filled with red frosting and fitted with a #104 decorating tip, hold the bag with the skinny end of the tip facing toward you, and the fat side of the tip going in toward the cake. Holding the bag vertically, and starting at the bottom of the cake, squeeze the pastry bag while going back and forth overlapping in 1-inch (2.5 cm)-wide rows while you go up the side of the cake tier. Continue overlapping the vertical ribbons; start again at the bottom of the cake right next to the first row and repeat the process all the way to the top edge of the 8-inch (20.5 cm) tier. Repeat this until both tiers are full of vertical ruffles.

7. Using the skinny part of the tip facing toward the outside of the cake, finish the cake by decorating the edge, going back and forth to create a border. Be sure to finish the border around the 8-inch (20.5 cm) cake as well.

Cookies and Cream Cow Cake Pops

IF I HAD ALL THE TIME IN THE WORLD, I'D LOVE TO MOLD AND DECORATE TINY COW FACES OUT OF CAKE. BUT I DON'T—AND WHO DOES? I'M A BUSY MOM WHO WORKS AROUND THE CLOCK JUST TO KEEP OUR HOUSEHOLD RUNNING SMOOTHLY. INSTEAD OF A TIME-CONSUMING COW, I CREATED A POP MADE FROM A SIMPLE DIPPED WHITE CAKE POP WITH DRAWN ON COW SPOTS. STANDING IN A BALE OF HAY, THERE'S NO DOUBT THAT THESE ARE COWS. MOOOOOO!

MAKES 40 CAKE POPS

INGREDIENTS

1 (18.25-OUNCE [517 G]) BOX DUNCAN HINES WHITE CAKE MIX

1 (3.4-OUNCE [110 G]) BOX JELL-O VANILLA INSTANT PUDDING AND PIE FILLING, DRY

1 CUP (235 ML) WATER

⅓ CUP (80 ML) OIL

4 LARGE EGGS

½ TO ¾ CUP (120 TO 175 ML) BUTTERCREAM FROSTING (PAGE 10)

1 PACKAGE OREO COOKIES, CRUSHED

3 (12-OUNCE [340 G]) PACKAGES WHITE CANDY MELTS

1 CUP BLACK CANDY MELTS

YOU WILL NEED

9 × 13-INCH (23 × 33 CM) BAKING PAN OR CASSEROLE DISH

40 (5-INCH [13 CM]) LOLLIPOP STICKS

DISPOSABLE PASTRY BAG

STYROFOAM

DIRECTIONS

1. Preheat the oven to 350°F (180°C). Coat the 9 × 13-inch (23 × 33 cm) baking pan with cooking spray, or grease and flour the pan, tapping out the excess flour. Set aside.

2. In a large bowl, and using an electric stand mixer fitted with a paddle attachment, beat the cake mix, pudding mix, water, oil and eggs on medium speed for 2 to 3 minutes, or until well blended. Scrape the sides of the bowl and mix again until all the ingredients are incorporated.

3. Pour the batter into the prepared cake pan. Place the pan in the preheated oven, and bake for 35 to 40 minutes, or until a toothpick inserted into the center comes out clean.

4. Remove the pan from the oven and place on a wire cooling rack for 25 to 30 minutes. Let cool completely before making the cake pops.

5. Mash up the cake and place in a large bowl. Using an electric stand mixer fitted with a paddle attachment, mix the cake, ½ to ¾ cup (130 to 175 ml) of icing, and the crushed Oreos on medium speed until moist and well blended and the mixture can be molded into a ball.

6. Measure and roll the mixture into 1 tablespoon-size balls and place on a cookie sheet. Refrigerate for 1 hour, or until firm.

7. Melt the white and black candy melts in separate microwave-safe bowls in 30-second increments at 40% power for about 1½ minutes, stirring as needed until smooth.

8. Remove the pops from the refrigerator. Dip each lollipop stick ¼ inch (6 mm) into melted candy. Insert the sticks into all the cake balls. (The melted candy will adhere the lollipop sticks to cake balls to prevent them from falling off the sticks when dipping). Proceed by dipping entire cake balls down into the melted candy.

9. Stand the pops up in a sheet of Styrofoam to dry for 5 to 10 minutes.

10. Pour the melted black candy into the pastry bag, and cut off a tiny hole at the tip with a pair of scissors. Decorate the cake pops by drawing cow spots in random splotches.

Strawberry Shortcakes in a Jar

THESE STRAWBERRY SHORTCAKES SERVED IN CANNING JARS ARE QUICK, EASY AND ADD GREAT PRESENTATION TO YOUR TABLE. TIE SCRAPS OF FABRIC AROUND THE LID AND, JUST BEFORE SERVING, TOP WITH COOL WHIP OR WHIPPED CREAM.

MAKES 12 TO 14 MINI SHORTCAKES

INGREDIENTS

6 CUPS (870 G) FRESH STRAWBERRIES, RINSED AND SLICED

⅔ CUP (134 G) PLUS 6 TABLESPOONS (75 G) GRANULATED SUGAR

4⅔ CUPS (737 G) BISQUICK BAKING MIX

1 CUP (235 ML) WHOLE MILK

6 TABLESPOONS (84 G) BUTTER OR MARGARINE, MELTED

16-OUNCE (575 ML) CONTAINER COOL WHIP OR WHIPPED CREAM, FOR GARNISH

YOU WILL NEED

1 NONSTICK COOKIE SHEET

COOKIE SCOOP

12 TO 14 SMALL GLASS CANNING JARS

RED GINGHAM FABRIC CUT IN STRIPS

DIRECTIONS

1. Preheat the oven to 425°F (220°C).

2. Place the strawberries in a large bowl and mix with ⅓ cup (67 g) of the sugar. Set aside.

3. In another large bowl, mix the Bisquick, milk and melted butter until a soft dough forms. Using the cookie scoop, measure the batter and place on an ungreased cookie sheet.

4. Bake for 9 to 10 minutes, or until golden brown. Remove the pan from the oven and place on a wire cooling rack until completely cool.

5. When ready to serve, place one shortcake biscuit in the bottom of each canning jar. Top with sliced strawberries, and garnish with Cool Whip or whipped cream.

Pigs in Mud

THESE LITTLE PIGGIES ARE IN HOG HEAVEN! TOP THESE CLASSIC TREATS WITH PINK CANDY MOLDED PIGS AND YOUR GUESTS WILL SQUEAL.

MAKES 24 TREATS

INGREDIENTS

1 (12-OUNCE [340 G]) PACKAGE PINK CANDY MELTS

2 CUPS (520 G) PEANUT BUTTER (I USE JIF)

1 (12-OUNCE [340 G]) PACKAGE SEMISWEET CHOCOLATE CHIPS (I USE NESTLÉ)

1 (12-OUNCE [340 G]) PACKAGE BUTTERSCOTCH CHIPS (I USE NESTLÉ)

1 TEASPOON VEGETABLE OIL

3 CUPS (115 G) SHOESTRING POTATO STICKS (I USE PIK-NIK)

YOU WILL NEED

PLASTIC PIG CANDY MOLD

COOKIE SCOOP

COOKIE SHEET

WAXED PAPER

DIRECTIONS

1. Melt the pink candy melts in a microwave-safe bowl in 30-second increments at 40% power for about 1½ minutes, stirring as needed until smooth. Fill the candy mold with the melted candy and chill until set, about 30 minutes. Remove the candies from the mold and set aside.

2. In a medium saucepan over low heat, combine the peanut butter, chocolate chips and butterscotch chips, stirring until melted. Stir in the oil. Remove from the heat.

3. Stir in the potato sticks and mix well until completely covered.

4. Using a cookie scoop, plop the mixture onto waxed paper and chill for 2 hours, or until set.

5. Place a pink candy pig on the top of each pile of mud.

Mini Cherry Pies with Lattice Crust

WHAT'S A FARM PARTY WITHOUT A CLASSIC CHERRY PIE? DON'T WORRY IF YOUR LATTICE CRUST ISN'T PERFECT; THESE PIES ARE SUPPOSED TO LOOK RUSTIC.

MAKES 12 CHERRY PIES

INGREDIENTS

2 STANDARD BOXES PILLSBURY PIE CRUST

2 (21-OUNCE [588 G]) CANS CHERRY PIE FILLING (I USE WILDERNESS)

YOU WILL NEED

ROLLING PIN

12 MINI PIE PANS

LARGE ROUND COOKIE CUTTER

COOKIE SHEET

DIRECTIONS

1. Preheat the oven to 425°F (220°C).

2. Remove the crusts from the pouches and roll out on a lightly floured surface. Using a large round cookie cutter, cut out a total of twelve pie crust circles. Press crusts into ungreased mini pie tins. Place the pies on a cookie sheet for stability. Roll the remaining crust into a rectangle, and using a sharp knife or pizza wheel, cut into thirty-six strips, about ½ to ¾ inch (1.3 to 2 cm) wide by 6 inches (15 cm) long.

3. Pick out twelve whole cherries and set them aside. Spoon about 4 teaspoons of the cherry pie filling into each pie crust. Lay the three strips pie crust across each pie, leaving equal space between them. Turn the pies around 90 degrees and place another three strips across the first strips. Gently weave the alternate strips up and under to form a basic lattice crust. Trim the excess pie crust with a knife, and press lightly to seal the edges.

4. Bake the pies for 18 to 20 minutes, or until crusts are golden brown. Cool completely in the pans, about 30 minutes. Place one of the reserved cherries on the top of each cherry pie.

Down on the Farm
Jenny Cookies

IS THERE ANYTHING CUTER THAN THESE FARM-SHAPED SUGAR COOKIES? HORSES, COWS, ROOSTERS, SHEEP AND PIGS, OH MY! KEEP THE DECORATING SIMPLE, NO NEED TO DRAW ON EVERY LAST ANIMAL DETAIL. WILTON TIPS 4 AND 18 MAKE DECORATING THESE ANIMALS SIMPLE, QUICK AND ADORABLE.

IF YOU WANT TO MAKE ALL SEVEN SUGAR COOKIES ON THE FARM TABLE AS THEY'RE PICTURED, YOU'LL NEED ONE BATCH OF BUTTERCREAM FROSTING (PAGE 10). FILL ONE BAG WITH WHITE BUTTERCREAM (YOU'LL NEED A LITTLE MORE WHITE FROSTING THAN THE REST OF THE COLORS), AND SET ASIDE. PLACE A SMALL AMOUNT OF BUTTERCREAM IN THREE SEPARATE SMALL BOWLS AND MIX ONE WITH YELLOW COLORING, ONE WITH ORANGE AND ONE WITH BLACK COLORING. PLACE EQUAL AMOUNTS OF THE REMAINING BUTTERCREAM IN FOUR SMALL BOWLS, AND MIX WITH THE APPROPRIATE COLORS; PINK, RED, GREEN AND BROWN. ATTACH WILTON DECORATING TIPS AND COUPLERS TO EACH OF THE PASTRY BAGS AND FILL WITH FROSTING. ALL EIGHT COLORS USE #4 WILTON TIPS, THE PINK FROSTING GETS BOTH #4 AND #2 TIPS, AND THE WHITE FROSTING GETS BOTH #4 AND #18 TIPS. IF YOU DON'T HAVE ENOUGH DECORATING TIPS FOR ALL THE BAGS, JUST CHANGE THEM OUT, WASH THEM AND PUT THEM IN ANOTHER BAG (USING COUPLERS MAKES CHANGING TIPS SO EASY). SEE THE COOKIE INGREDIENTS AND DIRECTIONS ON PAGE 12.

YOU WILL NEED

ROLLING PIN
2 NONSTICK COOKIE SHEETS
COOKIE SPATULA
HORSE COOKIE CUTTER
COW COOKIE CUTTER
ROOSTER COOKIE CUTTER
TRACTOR COOKIE CUTTER
BARN COOKIE CUTTER
SHEEP COOKIE CUTTER
PIG COOKIE CUTTER
8 DISPOSABLE PASTRY BAGS
8 #4 WILTON DECORATING TIPS
1 #18 WILTON DECORATING TIP
1 #2 WILTON DECORATING TIP
8 WILTON COUPLERS
AMERICOLOR SOFT GEL PASTE COLORS
TO MAKE RED, BROWN, BLACK, PINK,
ORNAGE, GREEN AND YELLOW

Horse Cookies

INGREDIENTS

BROWN BUTTERCREAM
BLACK BUTTERCREAM
YELLOW BUTTERCREAM

To decorate the horse cookies, use the pastry bag filled with brown frosting. Fitted with a #4 Wilton decorating tip, outline the entire body. Fill in the outline with brown frosting, running it vertically up and down from one side to the other until it is completely filled in. Using the pastry bag with yellow frosting and a #4 tip, make a mane and tail. Using the bag with black frosting and a #4 tip, give the horse hooves and an eye.

(continued)

Cow Cookies

INGREDIENTS
WHITE BUTTERCREAM
BLACK BUTTERCREAM
YELLOW BUTTERCREAM
RED BUTTERCREAM
PINK BUTTERCREAM

To decorate the cow cookies, use the pastry bag filled with white frosting, and fitted with a #4 Wilton decorating tip. Begin by outlining the cow's body, avoiding the hooves and nose. Fill in the outline with white frosting, running it vertically from one side to the other until it is completely filled in. Using the bag with black frosting and a #4 tip, create random and irregular cow spots by filling them in with frosting. Make each cow unique by giving her different spots. Continue using the black frosting and give the cow ears, nose, eyes and a tail. Using the bag with pink frosting and a #4 tip, make the udder. Draw a red frosting collar and a yellow bell using #4 tips.

Rooster Cookies

INGREDIENTS
YELLOW BUTTERCREAM
RED BUTTERCREAM
BROWN BUTTERCREAM
ORANGE BUTTERCREAM
GREEN BUTTERCREAM

To decorate the rooster cookies, use the pastry bag filled with yellow frosting, and fitted with a #4 Wilton decorating tip. Begin by outlining the rooster's front breast, then fill it in with yellow frosting, running it horizontally from one side to the other until it is completely filled in. Using the pastry bag with brown frosting, outline the rooster's bottom feathers and fill in with the same frosting running the lines across. Outline the remaining feathers with orange, red and green frosting using #4 tips, and running the lines as shown in the photo. Outline the rooster's head with red frosting and fill it in creating the rooster's wattle. Give the rooster an orange beak and feet, and a brown eye.

Tractor Cookies

INGREDIENTS
GREEN BUTTERCREAM
WHITE BUTTERCREAM
BLACK BUTTERCREAM
YELLOW BUTTERCREAM

To decorate the tractor cookies, use the pastry bag filled with green frosting, and fitted with a #4 Wilton decorating tip. Begin by outlining the tractor body, avoiding the wheels, window and roof. Fill in the outline with green frosting, running it vertically from top to the bottom until it is completely filled in. Using the white frosting and a #4 tip, run lines vertically to fill in the window. To create tractor tires, use the pastry bag filled with black frosting and #4 tip, and draw two to three fat circles, making sure to leave the middle empty. Fill the circle in with yellow frosting, and finish it off with black hubcaps. Continue using the black frosting to draw steering wheels and radiator grills.

Pig Cookies

INGREDIENTS
PINK BUTTERCREAM
BROWN BUTTERCREAM

To decorate the pig cookies, use the pastry bag filled with pink frosting and fitted with a #4 decorating tip. Outline the pig and fill it in with frosting, running it horizontally from one side to the other until the pig is completely filled in. Give the pig a squiggly pink buttercream tail and an eye with brown frosting.

Barn Cookies

INGREDIENTS
RED BUTTERCREAM
BROWN BUTTERCREAM
WHITE BUTTERCREAM
YELLOW BUTTERCREAM

To decorate the barn cookies, use the pastry bag filled with red frosting, and fitted with a #4 Wilton decorating tip. Begin by outlining the barn, then fill in the outline with frosting, running it horizontally from one side to the other until it is completely filled in. Outline the roof of the barn with brown frosting. Using the bag with yellow frosting and #4 tip, draw grass in front of the barn. Using the bag with white frosting and #2 tip, outline the barn doors and window.

Sheep Cookies

INGREDIENTS
WHITE BUTTERCREAM
BLACK BUTTERCREAM

To decorate the sheep cookies, use the pastry bag filled with white frosting, and fitted with a #18 Wilton decorating tip. Fill in the body of the sheep with swirly fluffy mounds that resemble the sheep's wool, making sure to avoid the head and legs. Using the pastry bag filled with black frosting and #4 tip, outline the sheep's head and fill it in diagonally. Give the sheep black legs and the eye with a dot of white frosting.

8

Shipwrecked

WHEN MY SON, HUDSON, TURNED FOUR, WE CELEBRATED WITH A PETER PAN PARTY ON THE BEACH. INVITES WERE SENT AS MESSAGES IN A BOTTLE, ROLLED LIKE A SCROLL INSIDE A BOTTLE FILLED WITH SAND, SHELLS AND A RED FEATHER (PETER PAN'S SIGNATURE HAT DETAIL). HUDSON DRESSED AS PETER, ALLY WAS WENDY, I WAS INDIAN PRINCESS TIGER LILY AND MY HUSBAND SURPRISED US BY DRESSING AS CAPTAIN HOOK.

NOT ALL KIDS LOVE PETER PAN, BUT MOST LOVE PIRATES. THIS THEME DOESN'T HAVE TO BE COSTLY—YOU CAN GATHER ITEMS AT SECONDHAND STORES, GARAGE SALES AND GOODWILL. I SCORED AN OLD ROUND TOP TRUNK (PERFECT FOR A TREASURE CHEST) AT AN ESTATE SALE AROUND THE CORNER FROM MY HOUSE FOR $10. I PICKED UP A FEW OLD PETER PAN STORY-BOOKS AND INEXPENSIVE SHEETS AT THE LOCAL THRIFT SHOP AND TUCKED THEM IN MY NOTORIOUS RUBBERMAID PARTY BINS.

When it came time for party prep, I shredded the ends and sides of fabric to give them a shipwrecked look, then gathered and hung them together from a wood beam to create a photo backdrop for party guests. I cut triangles from the old Peter Pan storybooks, punched holes in them, strung them with jute rope, and created Peter Pan party garlands. Inspired by the fabrics of Captain Hook's burgundy velvet coat and the props you'd see in the dark Pirates of the Caribbean boat ride in Disneyland, I found an old brass candelabra, gold vases and tarnished silver platters at secondhand stores. In my local party store's Halloween section, I picked up a skeleton head, shredded fabric for a table cover and a bendable skeleton for a fun cake topper. It was such a fun party—one of my favorites.

SETTING THE TABLE

Kids love to believe in buried treasure, so build desserts around them. Try a cupcake with a chocolate peanut butter cup candy baked into the bottom and call it a buried treasure cupcake. Fill Ritz crackers with peanut butter, dip them in golden yellow candy melts, sprinkle with edible glitter, and call them gold doubloons. Sugar cookies round out the dessert table. Shape them as treasure maps, crossbones, pirate ships, swords and parrots. And Rice Krispie treats molded into eye patches or attached to a stick work double duty as an edible photo prop.

Build your table vertically, with a couple of old wood crates and boxes with the shredded fabric underneath. A mixture of the handmade gold wood stands and tarnished silver trays can complete the dessert display pieces. Here, peanut butter cracker gold doubloon cookies are set inside an old treasure chest. Place the cake on an old wood candleholder with Mr. Skeleton sitting on top with a handful of pirate treasure. Line the tarnished silver trays with assorted cookies and stand the Rice Krispie treat eye patches in an old wood box filled with sand (to cover the Styrofoam). Place flowers in old glass bottles and colored metal canisters to add pops of color. Lastly, try to find an old trunk and place it at the foot of the table, like an actual pirate treasure chest. With a trunk, a child can easily stand on top while blowing out his candles. (It's also a great place to stash take-home boxes or goodie bags!)

SHIPWRECKED DESSERTS

- ♥ **Shiver Me Timbers Cake**
- ♥ **Gold Doubloons PB Cookies**
- ♥ **Cannonball Cake Pops**
- ♥ **Buried Treasure Cupcakes**
- ♥ **Eye Patch Rice Krispie Treats**
- ♥ **Captains Parrot Cookies**
- ♥ **Swashbuckling Sword Sugar Cookies**
- ♥ **Treasure Map Cookies**
- ♥ **Pirate Ship Sugar Cookies**
- ♥ **Crossbones Sugar Cookies**

Shiver Me Timbers Cake

Note: This cake is large and uses four boxes of cake mix. The bowl of a standard electric stand mixer is not large enough to hold ingredients for four cakes. You may have to mix the batter and bake in two or three batches.

MAKES ONE 8-INCH (20.5 CM) AND 10-INCH (25.5 CM) TIERED CAKE

INGREDIENTS

4 (18.25-OUNCE [517 G]) BOXES DUNCAN HINES DEVIL'S FOOD CAKE MIX

4 (3.4-OUNCE [110 G]) BOXES JELL-O CHOCOLATE INSTANT PUDDING AND PIE FILLING, DRY

4 CUPS (945 ML) WATER

1 ⅓ CUPS (320 ML) OIL

16 LARGE EGGS

3 BATCHES CHOCOLATE BUTTERCREAM FROSTING (PAGE 10)

AMERICOLOR BLACK SOFT GEL PASTE COLOR

GRAHAM CRACKER CRUMBS

YOU WILL NEED

2 (10 × 2-INCH [25.5 × 5 CM]) AND 2 (8 × 2-INCH [20.5 × 5 CM]) ROUND NONSTICK CAKE PANS

CAKE CUTTER OR LONG, SERRATED KNIFE

2 ROUND CARDBOARD OR PLASTIC CAKE BOARDS

OFFSET ANGLED SPATULA

CAKE SCRAPER

CAKE DECORATING TURNTABLE

POINTED, ANGLED OFFSET SPATULA

6 (¼-INCH [6 MM]-THICK) DOWELS OR THICK PLASTIC STRAWS

LARGE, FLAT SPATULA

DIRECTIONS

1. Preheat the oven to 350°F (180°C). Coat the 8-inch (20.5 cm) and 10-inch (25.5 cm) round nonstick cake pans with cooking spray or grease and flour the pans, tapping out the excess flour. Set the prepared pans aside.

2. In a large bowl, and using an electric stand mixer fitted with a paddle attachment, beat the cake mix, pudding mix, water, oil and eggs on medium speed for 2 to 3 minutes, or until well blended. Scrape the sides of the bowl and mix again until all the ingredients are incorporated.

3. Pour batter into the prepared cake pans, filling each one approximately three-quarters full.

4. Place the pans in the preheated oven, on the middle rack. Bake 8-inch (20.5 cm) cakes for 30 to 35 minutes, and 10-inch (25.5 cm) cakes for 35 to 40 minutes, or until a toothpick inserted into the center comes out clean. Depending on the size of your oven, cakes may need to be baked in two or three batches.

5. Remove the pans from the oven and place on wire cooling racks for 25 to 30 minutes. Run a knife around the edges of the cakes, flip the pans over and gently extract the cakes. Return the cakes to the wire racks and finish cooling completely before frosting and decorating. After the layers are cooled, freeze or refrigerate the cakes for 1 hour before decorating to reduce crumbs and make for a smoother icing process.

6. Meanwhile, make the three batches of chocolate buttercream frosting. Add black food coloring to the frosting until it reaches the desired shade.

TO ASSEMBLE AND DECORATE THE CAKE

1. Before decorating, trim the crowns from the cake tops with a cake cutter or long, serrated knife so they are flat and even.

2. Place one of the 10-inch (25.5 cm) cakes on a cake board. Using the angled cake spatula, spread about ¾ cup (175 ml) of frosting evenly across the top of the cake layer. Place the second 10-inch (25.5 cm) cake on top of the first, with the cut side on the bottom. Use the angled cake spatula to cover the cake completely with a very thin layer of icing (or crumb coat) to help reduce the amount of crumbs in the final coat of icing. Set the two-tiered 10-inch (25.5 cm) cake aside.

3. Repeat this process with the 8-inch (20.5 cm) cake layers. Once the same process has been completed on the 8-inch (20.5 cm) cake layers, allow them to dry for 1 hour, or until the icing crusts.

4. Frost the top and sides of the 10-inch tier (25.5 cm) with a thicker layer of black buttercream frosting, and use the cake scraper to smooth. Place the tier on a rotating cake turntable. Create a swirled pattern by gently placing the tip of the pointed, angled spatula at the bottom of the cake. Slowly spin the turntable while moving the spatula up the side of the cake to the top edge. Set the tier aside.

5. Repeat step 4 with the 8-inch (20.5 cm) tier. Make sure the top tier has a nice smooth icing finish before decorating.

6. Return the 10-inch (125.5 cm) tier to the turntable.

7. Create supports for the smaller cake to sit atop the larger cake by placing the dowels into the top of the 10-inch (25.5 cm) cake. Insert the first dowel into the cake and use a pen to mark the dowel at the point where it just comes to the top of the cake. Remove the dowel and cut it at that mark. Cut five to six additional dowels or straws to the same length and place them in a circle, approximately 2 inches (5 cm) from the center of the cake, and evenly spaced. Using a large, flat spatula, carefully center and place the 6-inch (15 cm) cake on top of the 10-inch (25.5 cm) cake.

8. Finish the swirl pattern on the tops of the tiers by pressing the tip of the pointed angled spatula to the outside edge and moving inward while spinning the turntable.

9. Sprinkle the graham cracker crumbs along the outside edge of the 10-inch (25.5 cm) tier, and on top of the 8-inch (20.5 cm) tier, being careful not to get any on the sides of the frosted cake.

10. Decorate the top of the cake with plastic skeleton, jewels and gold coins.

Cannonball Cake Pops

HANDS DOWN, OREO CAKE POPS ARE MY MOST POPULAR AND REQUESTED CAKE POP FLAVOR. OFTEN PEOPLE WONDER WHY THEY'RE SO CHOCOLATY, MOIST AND CREAMY—IT'S THE MIXTURE OF CHOCOLATE CAKE AND CLASSIC OREO COOKIES COMBINED WITH A BIT OF MY BUTTERCREAM. THESE MINI TREATS ARE SO DELICIOUS THAT GUESTS COME BACK FOR TWO OR THREE.

MAKES 40 CAKE POPS

INGREDIENTS

1 (18.25-OUNCE [517 G]) BOX DUNCAN HINES DEVIL'S FOOD CAKE MIX

1 (3.4-OUNCE [110 G]) BOX JELL-O CHOCOLATE INSTANT PUDDING AND PIE FILLING, DRY

1 CUP (235 ML) WATER

⅓ CUP (80 ML) OIL

4 LARGE EGGS

½ TO ¾ CUP (120 TO 175 ML) BUTTERCREAM FROSTING (PAGE 10)

1 (14.3-OUNCE [405 G]) PACKAGE OREO COOKIES (ABOUT 36), CRUSHED

3 (12-OUNCE [340 G]) PACKAGES BLACK CANDY MELTS

BLACK SUGAR SPRINKLES

YOU WILL NEED

9 × 13-INCH (23 × 33 CM) BAKING PAN OR CASSEROLE DISH

40 (5-INCH [13 CM]) LOLLIPOP STICKS

STYROFOAM

DIRECTIONS

1. Preheat the oven to 350°F (180°C). Coat the 9 × 13-inch (23 × 33 cm) baking pan with cooking spray, or grease and flour pan, tapping out the excess flour. Set aside.

2. In a large bowl, and using an electric stand mixer fitted with a paddle attachment, beat the cake mix, pudding mix, water, oil and eggs on medium speed for 2 to 3 minutes, or until well blended. Scrape the sides of the bowl and mix again until all the ingredients are incorporated.

3. Pour the batter into the prepared cake pan. Place the pan in the preheated oven and bake for 35 to 40 minutes, or until a toothpick inserted into the center comes out clean.

4. Remove the pan from the oven and place on a wire cooling rack for 25 to 30 minutes. Let cool completely before making the cake pops.

5. Mash up the cake and place in a large bowl. Using an electric stand mixer fitted with a paddle attachment, mix the cake, Oreos and ½ to ¾ cup (120 to 175 ml) of frosting on medium speed until well blended and the mixture can be molded into a ball.

6. Measure and roll mixture into 1 tablespoon-size balls and place on a cookie sheet. Refrigerate for 1 hour, or until firm.

7. Melt the candy melts in a microwave-safe bowl in 30-second increments, for about 2½ minutes at 40% power, stirring as needed until smooth. Remove the bowl from the microwave.

8. Remove the pops from the refrigerator. Dip each lollipop stick ¼ inch (6 mm) into the melted candy. Insert the sticks into all the cake balls. (The melted candy will adhere the lollipop sticks to cake balls to prevent them from falling off the sticks when dipping). Proceed to dip entire cake balls down into melted candy. Use a spoon to sprinkle black sugar sprinkles over the cake pops until completely covered.

9. Stand the pops up in a sheet of Styrofoam to dry.

Gold Doubloons PB Cookies

PINT-SIZED PIRATES LOVE THESE CRUNCHY PEANUT BUTTER GOLD DOUBLOON COOKIES. DISPLAY THEM IN A WOODEN CHEST TO GIVE THEM A REALISTIC BURIED-TREASURE LOOK.

MAKES 17 TREATS

INGREDIENTS

1 PACKAGE (SLEEVE OF 34) RITZ CRACKERS

1 CUP (260 G) SMOOTH PEANUT BUTTER (I USE JIF)

2 (12-OUNCE [340 G]) PACKAGES YELLOW CANDY MELTS (PLUS A FEW BROWN/CHOCOLATE MELTS TO MAKE IT LOOK GOLDEN)

2 TABLESPOONS GOLD DISCO DUST

YOU WILL NEED

DISPOSABLE PASTRY BAG

PAINT- OR CRAFT BRUSH

WAXED PAPER

DIRECTIONS

1. Turn the Ritz crackers upside down on a cookie sheet. Fill the pastry bag with peanut butter. Cut small tip from pastry bag and pipe a dollop of peanut butter on half the crackers. Place the remaining crackers on top to make sandwiches.

2. Melt the candy melts in a microwave-safe bowl in 30-second increments at 40% power for about 2½ minutes, stirring as needed until smooth.

3. Using a fork, dip the crackers into the melted candy. Dip a paint- or craft brush into Disco Dust and gently tap to dust cookies while the coating is still tacky. Place the finished treats on waxed paper to dry.

Buried Treasure Cupcakes

YOUR GUESTS WILL BITE INTO THESE RICH CHOCOLATE CUPCAKES AND FIND A HIDDEN PEANUT BUTTER CUP TREASURE BURIED IN THE BOTTOM. NOT A FAN OF PEANUT BUTTER? SWAP YOUR MINIATURE PEANUT BUTTER CUPS FOR A FEW PIECES OF YOUR FAVORITE CHOCOLATE BAR, CHOPPED UP.

MAKES 24 CUPCAKES

INGREDIENTS

1 (12-OUNCE [340 G]) PACKAGE WHITE CANDY MELTS

1 (18.25-OUNCE [517 G]) BOX DUNCAN HINES TRIPLE CHOCOLATE CAKE MIX

1 (3.4-OUNCE [110 G]) BOX JELL-O CHOCOLATE INSTANT PUDDING AND PIE FILLING, DRY

1 CUP (235 ML) WATER

⅓ CUP (80 ML) OIL

4 LARGE EGGS

1 PACKAGE (ABOUT 24) REESE'S MINI PEANUT BUTTER CUPS

1 BATCH BUTTERCREAM FROSTING (PAGE 10)

BLACK SANDING SUGAR

YOU WILL NEED

CHOCOLATE MOLD OF SKULL, FOR DECORATION

2 STANDARD-SIZE CUPCAKE TRAYS

24 STANDARD PAPER CUPCAKE LINERS

COOKIE SCOOP

2 DISPOSABLE PASTRY BAGS

WILTON 1A TIP

DIRECTIONS

1. Melt the candy melts in a microwave-safe bowl in 30-second increments at 40% power for about 1½ minutes, stirring as needed until smooth. Pour melted candy into disposable pastry bag and trim tip with scissors. Fill the candy mold with the melted candy and chill until set, about 30 minutes. Remove from the mold and set aside.

2. Preheat the oven to 350°F (180°C). Line the cupcake trays with paper cupcake liners. Set the prepared trays aside.

3. In a large bowl, and using an electric stand mixer fitted with a paddle attachment, beat the cake mix, pudding mix, water, oil and eggs on medium speed for 2 to 3 minutes, or until well blended. Scrape down the sides of the bowl, and mix again until all the ingredients are incorporated.

4. Using a cookie scoop, place some cake batter (about one-third full) into each paper liner, place one Reese's peanut butter cup in each and top with more batter to fill the liner about two-thirds full total, dividing evenly between the cupcake trays.

5. Bake the cupcakes for 18 to 20 minutes, or until the tops spring back when lightly touched. Remove the cupcakes from the oven and place the trays on wire cooling racks for 15 minutes. Take the cupcakes out of the trays and allow them to cool completely on the wire racks before decorating.

6. Cut off the tip of a decorating bag and drop a Wilton 1A tip down inside. Fill the bag with buttercream. Pipe a buttercream ring around the outer circle of each cupcake, building the layers and moving toward the center until you reach the top.

7. Place the black sanding sugar in a shallow bowl. Dip the cupcake tops into the sugar, making sure it adheres to the buttercream.

8. Remove the candy skulls from the mold and place one on top of each Buried Treasure cupcake.

Eye Patch Rice Krispie Treats

THESE SUGARED RICE KRISPIE TREATS ARE A FUN PHOTO BOOTH PROP. GRAB A POP OFF THE DESSERT TABLE AND HEAD STRAIGHT TO THE PARTY PHOTO AREA AND POSE WITH YOUR TREAT.

MAKES 12 TO 15 TREATS

INGREDIENTS

VEGETABLE SPRAY

3 TABLESPOONS (42 G) BUTTER OR MARGARINE

1 (10-OUNCE [280 G]) PACKAGE MINI MARSHMALLOWS (4 CUPS)

BLACK FOOD COLORING

6 CUPS (250 G) RICE KRISPIES CEREAL

BLACK SANDING SUGAR

YOU WILL NEED

9 × 13-INCH (23 × 33 CM) BAKING PAN OR CASSEROLE DISH

FOOTBALL OR OVAL COOKIE CUTTER

12 TO 15 LOLLIPOP OR COOKIE STICKS

DISPOSABLE PASTRY BAG

WILTON COUPLER

#4 WILTON DECORATING TIP

STYROFOAM

DIRECTIONS

1. Lightly oil or spray the 9 × 13-inch (23 × 33 cm) baking pan or with vegetable spray.

2. In a large saucepan over low heat, melt the butter. Add the marshmallows and stir until melted and smooth. Remove the pan from the heat. Add black food coloring and stir again.

3. Add the Rice Krispies and stir until completely coated. Pat into the prepared baking pan and let cool completely to set.

4. Once set, cut out pirate patch shapes, using the football or oval cookie cutter (or manipulate a circle cutter into patch shape).

5. Insert one lollipop stick into the bottom of each patch.

6. Dip the patches in a bowl filled with black sanding sugar, or sprinkle sugar, covering the patches completely. Place on waxed paper.

7. To decorate the patches, place a small amount of white buttercream frosting in a disposable pastry bag fitted with a #4 Wilton decorating tip. Place an X in the middle of each pirate patch.

8. Insert the treats into the Styrofoam and cover with sand.

Shipwrecked Jenny Cookies

YO-HO-HO, AND A TABLE FULL OF BRIGHT COLORFUL COOKIES AND SWASHBUCKLING FUN! EVERY PIRATE NEEDS A PARROT, A SWORD AND A TREASURE MAP—PREFERABLY IN BUTTERCREAM. THESE FESTIVE COOKIES ALSO MAKE GREAT PARTY FAVORS. DRAW THE NAME AND AGE OF THE BIRTHDAY CHILD ON THE PIRATE SHIP COOKIES, THEN PACKAGE THEM UP IN CELLOPHANE BAGS.

IF YOU WANT TO MAKE ALL FIVE SUGAR COOKIES ON THE PIRATE PARTY DESSERT TABLE AS THEY'RE PICTURED, MAKE ONE BATCH OF BUTTERCREAM FROSTING AS DIRECTED ON PAGE 10 AND TINT EACH WITH THE APPROPRIATE COLORS. ATTACH WILTON DECORATING TIPS AND COUPLERS TO EACH OF THE PASTRY BAGS AND FILL WITH FROSTING. LOTS OF DIFFERENT COLORS ARE USED FOR THE PIRATE COOKIES, BUT IT'S EASIER THAN IT LOOKS. IF YOU TINT THE BUTTERCREAM AND FILL EACH PASTRY BAG AHEAD OF TIME, YOU'LL BE AHEAD OF THE GAME. PLUS, YOU'LL ONLY NEED A SMALL AMOUNT FOR FOUR OF THE COLORS (ORANGE, YELLOW, GREEN AND BLUE). THESE COOKIES ALSO USE A NUMBER OF PASTRY BAGS—SEVEN IN ALL—SO IT'S BETTER IN THE LONG RUN TO USE DISPOSABLE BAGS AND THROW THEM AWAY WHEN YOU'RE DONE. I ONLY USE TWO DIFFERENT SIZE WILTON TIPS WITH THESE COOKIES—#3 AND #4, BUT I USE ONE IN EVERY BAG. IF YOU DON'T HAVE ENOUGH DECORATING TIPS FOR ALL THE BAGS, JUST CHANGE THEM OUT, WASH THEM, AND PUT THEM IN ANOTHER BAG (USING COUPLERS MAKES CHANGING TIPS SO EASY). YOU'LL ALSO BE MAKING JUST ONE BATCH OF SUGAR COOKIE DOUGH AND USING IT FOR ALL FIVE COOKIE SHAPES AND BAKING THEM IN THE OVEN AT THE SAME TIME. SEE PAGE 12 IN BASICS CHAPTER FOR COOKIE INGREDIENTS AND DIRECTIONS.

MAKES ABOUT 24 COOKIES

YOU WILL NEED

ROLLING PIN
2 NONSTICK COOKIE SHEETS
COOKIE SPATULA
PARROT COOKIE CUTTER
SWORD COOKIE CUTTER
BEACH TOWEL COOKIE CUTTER (FOR TREASURE MAPS)
PIRATE SHIP OR BOAT COOKIE CUTTER
SKULL AND CROSSBONES COOKIE CUTTER
7 TO 8 DISPOSABLE PASTRY BAGS
5 #4 WILTON DECORATING TIPS
3 #3 WILTON DECORATING TIPS
5 WILTON COUPLERS
AMERICOLOR SOFT GEL PASTE COLORS TO MAKE BLACK, BROWN, BLUE, RED, YELLOW, GREEN, ORANGE
DISCO DUST

Swashbuckling Sword Sugar Cookies

INGREDIENTS

BLACK BUTTERCREAM
BROWN BUTTERCREAM

To decorate the sword cookies, use prefilled pastry bags filled with black and brown buttercream and #4 decorating tips. Outline the body of the sword with black buttercream. Fill in the outline with black frosting, running it horizontally until completely filled in. Create the sword handle using the pastry bag with brown buttercream.

(continued)

Captains Parrot Cookies

INGREDIENTS

WHITE BUTTERCREAM

RED BUTTERCREAM

ORANGE BUTTERCREAM

YELLOW BUTTERCREAM

BLUE BUTTERCREAM

BLACK BUTTERCREAM

To decorate the parrot cookies, place small amounts of orange, yellow, green and blue buttercream frosting in separate pastry bags fitted with #4 Wilton decorating tips. Use prefilled pastry bags filled with black, red and white buttercream, and fitted with #4 decorating tips. Following the photo opposite, outline the parrot's head and a portion of his body with red buttercream. Fill in the outlines with red frosting, running it horizontally from one edge of the outlines to the other, until completely filled in. Using the pastry bags with orange, yellow and green buttercream, create wing feathers with vertical lines of icing. Outline the tail feathers with blue buttercream and fill in. Give the parrot an eye and beak with black and white buttercream.

Pirate Ship Sugar Cookies

INGREDIENTS

BROWN BUTTERCREAM

WHITE BUTTERCREAM

BLACK BUTTERCREAM

RED BUTTERCREAM

To decorate the pirate ship cookies, use prefilled pastry bags filled with white and brown buttercream and #4 decorating tips, and pastry bags filled with black and red buttercream fitted with #3 decorating tips. Following the photo opposite, outline the bottom of the pirate ship with brown buttercream. Fill in the outline with brown frosting, running it vertically from one edge of the outline to the other, until completely filled in. Create a mast and poles with brown buttercream. Using the pastry bag with black buttercream, outline the sail. Fill in the sail with white buttercream running it horizontally until filled in. Finish decorating the cookies as shown in the photo with red and white buttercream and a big black X.

Treasure Map Cookies

INGREDIENTS

WHITE BUTTERCREAM

RED BUTTERCREAM

BLACK BUTTERCREAM

To decorate the treasure map cookies, use a prefilled pastry bag filled with white buttercream and #4 decorating tip, and pastry bags filled with black and red buttercream fitted with #3 decorating tips. Following the photo opposite, outline the treasure map with white buttercream. Fill in the outline with white frosting, running it vertically from one edge of the outline to the other, until completely filled in. Using the pastry bag with black buttercream, draw broken lines to mark the directions. Sprinkle a little Disco Dust at the end of the course. Use the pastry bag with red buttercream for X marks the spot.

Crossbones Sugar Cookies

INGREDIENTS

WHITE BUTTERCREAM

BLACK BUTTERCREAM

To decorate the crossbones cookies, use prefilled pastry bags filled with white buttercream and #4 decorating tip, and another with black buttercream and #3 decorating tip. Following the photo opposite, outline the bones and skull with white buttercream. Fill in the bones outline with white frosting, running it diagonally until completely filled in. Fill in the skull outline horizontally. Create eyes, nose and mouth with black buttercream and #3 decorating tip.

9

Campout

GROWING UP, I TOOK A LOT OF CAMPING TRIPS WITH MY FAMILY. I LOVED PICKING OUT THE BEST CAMPSITE, SETTING UP OUR LITTLE HOME AWAY FROM HOME AND THEN GETTING READY TO RELAX FOR THE REST OF THE WEEKEND. LOTS OF CARD GAMES PLAYED AT THE PICNIC TABLE, S'MORES ROASTED OVER THE FIRE PIT AND MY FAVORITE—THE ACTIVITIES THE PARK RANGERS PUT ON FOR KIDS. WE'D SPEND THE WEEKEND COLLECTING OUR BADGES FOR TAKING HIKES, LEARNING ABOUT NATURE AND PICKING UP TRASH AROUND THE CAMPGROUND. IT WAS CHEAP, FUN AND WE WERE SO EXHAUSTED BY THE END OF THE DAY THAT WE FELL FAST ASLEEP IN OUR TENTS WITHOUT A SINGLE BEDTIME BATTLE WITH OUR PARENTS.

BUT WITH TIME AND AGE, MY FEELINGS TOWARD THE GREAT OUTDOORS HAVE CHANGED A BIT. INSTEAD OF PACKING UP EVERYTHING YOU OWN TO ROUGH IT FOR A FEW DAYS OUTSIDE IN THE WILDERNESS, WHY NOT JUST THROW A CAMP-OUT PARTY? INVITE FRIENDS TO EXPERIENCE THE JOYS OF THE GREAT OUTDOORS BUT WITH THE COMFORT OF GREAT DESSERT, COMPANY AND THE CONFIDENCE IN KNOWING YOU'LL SLEEP COMFORTABLY IN YOUR OWN BED THAT NIGHT.

When you're camping, you're also sitting around eating. What better place to have a dessert table? There are so many creative ideas for camp-themed desserts—especially with marshmallows or s'mores. So to begin the campout dessert table, start with a bag of jumbo Jet-Puffed marshmallows and a handful of real tree branches and sticks. (This is a great job for a kid: Send them on a nature hunt for sticks, and in exchange, they'll get a fun s'mores dessert.) Then poke a stick into each jumbo marshmallow and dip the ends into melted chocolate and top them with crushed graham crackers. Voilà! s'mores on a stick.

Next, make a homemade batch of trail mix, using your kids' favorite candies and cereal. Hikers always need a good snack out on the trail. Sugar cookies can be shaped as teepee tents, squirrels, moose heads, canoes and pinecones. To complete the table, make a chocolate cake and stuff it with a creamy marshmallow filling. Then make a tiny tent from a scrap of fabric, five sticks, and some twine. Using a chocolate mold, make a chocolate sign and then pipe Happy Trails in buttercream.

SETTING THE TABLE

For my campout dessert table, start with an old wood picnic table. (I love the texture of the wood and the rusty metal legs.) Pick up flannel at your local fabric store and fold it to form a makeshift table runner, for a pop of plaid. Desserts can be set atop tree rounds and stumps, adding a bit of texture and nature to the table. The s'mores on sticks can be placed inside an old metal camp stove, and the cake can be set on a vintage tin picnic basket. For added color, fill a vintage thermos and tins with colorful flowers. Add a few old lanterns to the table for an added camp feel and fun prop. The great thing about this camping table is the variety of color and display pieces. Just about anything outdoorsy works.

CAMPOUT DESSERTS

- ♥ Happy Campers Cake
- ♥ Acorn Donuts
- ♥ Happy Trails Mix
- ♥ Campground Cookies
- ♥ Don't Feed the Bears Brownie Pops
- ♥ Kumbaya Cupcakes
- ♥ Great Outdoors S'mores
- ♥ S'mores on a Stick
- ♥ Canoe Cookies
- ♥ Teepee Tent Cookies
- ♥ Moose Head Cookies
- ♥ Squirrel Cookies
- ♥ Pinecone Cookies

Happy Campers Cake

LIKE MANY OF MY CAKES, THE HAPPY CAMPERS CAKE HIDES A MOUTHWATERING SECRET BENEATH ALL THAT BUTTERCREAM FROSTING. JUST LIKE A GIANT S'MORE, THIS SCRUMPTIOUS CAKE MADE WITH MOIST DEVIL'S FOOD CHOCOLATE LAYERS IS FILLED WITH THE FLUFFIEST MARSHMALLOW FILLING. DON'T LET THE ROWS AND ROWS OF VANILLA BUTTERCREAM SCALLOPS INTIMIDATE YOU. THEY'RE AMAZINGLY SIMPLE TO PRODUCE USING A SIMPLE DECORATING TECHNIQUE. AFTER FINISHING THE FIRST ROW, YOU'LL BE WHIPPING OUT BUTTERCREAM SCALLOPS—AND YOUR GUESTS WILL BE CONVINCED THAT YOU WORKED ON THIS CAKE ALL DAY.

Note: This cake is large and uses three boxes of cake mix. The bowl of a standard electric stand mixer is not large enough to hold ingredients for three cakes. You may have to mix the batter and bake the cake in two batches.

MAKES ONE 8-INCH (20.5 CM) AND 9-INCH (23 CM) TIERED CAKE

INGREDIENTS

3 (18.25-OUNCE [517 G])BOXES DUNCAN HINES DEVIL'S FOOD CAKE MIX

3 (3.4-OUNCE [110 G]) BOXES JELL-O CHOCOLATE INSTANT PUDDING AND PIE FILLING, DRY

3 CUPS (710 ML) WATER

1 CUP (235 ML) OIL

12 LARGE EGGS

MARSHMALLOW FILLING

3 BATCHES BUTTERCREAM FROSTING (SEE PAGE 10)

AMERICOLOR YELLOW SOFT GEL PASTE COLOR

MARSHMALLOW FILLING INGREDIENTS

4 TABLESPOONS (57 G) SALTED BUTTER, AT ROOM TEMPERATURE

1 CUP (125 G) CONFECTIONERS' SUGAR

2 TEASPOON PURE VANILLA EXTRACT

3 TABLESPOONS (45 ML) WHOLE MILK

1 CUP (235 ML) MARSHMALLOW CREME (JET-PUFFED MARSHMALLOW CREME)

DIRECTIONS

1. Preheat the oven to 350°F (180°C). Coat the 8-inch (20.5 cm) and 9-inch (23 cm) round cake pans with cooking spray, or grease and flour the pans, tapping out the excess flour. Set the prepared pans aside.

2. In a large bowl, and using an electric stand mixer fitted with a paddle attachment, beat the cake mix, pudding mix, water, oil and eggs on medium speed for 2 to 3 minutes, or until well blended. Scrape the sides of the bowl and mix again until all the ingredients are incorporated.

3. Pour the batter into the prepared cake pans, filling each one approximately three-quarters full. Place the pans in the preheated oven, using the middle rack. Bake the 8-inch (20.5 cm) cakes and 9-inch (23 cm) cakes for 30 to 35 minutes, or until a toothpick inserted into the center comes out clean. Depending on your oven size, cakes may need to be baked in seperate batches.

4. Remove the pans from the oven and place on wire cooling racks for 25 to 30 minutes. Run a knife around the edges of the cakes, flip the pans over, and gently extract cakes. Return the cakes to the wire racks and finish cooling completely before frosting and decorating. After the layers are cooled, freeze or refrigerate the cakes for 1 hour before decorating to reduce crumbs to make for a smoother icing process.

5. Meanwhile, make the three batches of buttercream frosting. Add yellow food coloring to the frosting until it reaches the desired shade.

6. Make the marshmallow filling and set aside.

FOR THE MARSHMALLOW FILLING

1. In a large bowl, and using an electric stand mixer fitted with a paddle attachment, beat the butter until light and fluffy.

(continued)

YOU WILL NEED

2 (8 × 2-INCH [20.5 × 5 CM]) AND 2 (9 × 2-INCH [23 × 5 CM]) ROUND NONSTICK CAKE PANS

CAKE CUTTER OR LONG, SERRATED KNIFE

2 ROUND CARDBOARD OR PLASTIC CAKE BOARDS

OFFSET ANGLED SPATULA

5 (¼-INCH [6 MM]-THICK) DOWELS OR THICK PLASTIC STRAWS

LARGE, FLAT SPATULA

CAKE DECORATING TURNTABLE

1 LARGE PASTRY BAG

#10 WILTON DECORATING TIP

1 WILTON COUPLER

2. Add ½ cup (62.5 g) of confectioners' sugar and mix until combined. Add the vanilla and 1 tablespoon of milk and beat until smooth. Add remaining ½ cup (62.5 g) of confectioners' sugar and 2 tablespoons (30 ml) of milk and beat again, scraping the sides of the bowl with a rubber spatula as needed.

3. Add the marshmallow creme (hint: spray the measuring cup first with vegetable spray so the marshmallow creme will come out easily), and mix until light and fluffy. Refrigerate until ready to use.

TO ASSEMBLE AND DECORATE THE CAKE

1. Before decorating, trim the crowns from the cake tops with a cake cutter or long, serrated knife so they are flat and even.

2. Place one of the 9-inch (23 cm) cakes on a cake board. Using the angled cake spatula, spread about 1 cup (235 ml) of marshmallow filling evenly across the top of the cake layer. Place the second 9-inch (23 cm) cake on top of the first, with the cut side on the bottom. Use the angled cake spatula to cover the cake completely with a very thin layer of icing (or crumb coat) to help reduce the amount of crumbs in the final coat of icing. Set the 2-tiered 9-inch (23 cm) cake aside.

3. Repeat this process with the 8-inch (20.5 cm) cake layers, using the remaining marshmallow filling between the layers, and icing the sides and top of the cake. Once the same process has been completed on the 8-inch (20.5 cm) cake layers, allow them to dry for 1 hour, or until the icing crusts.

4. Create supports for the smaller cake to sit atop the larger cake by placing the dowels into the top of the 9-inch (23 cm) cake. Insert the first dowel into the cake and use a pen to mark the dowel at the point where it just comes to the top of the cake. Remove the dowel and cut it at that mark. Cut three to four additional dowels or straws to the same length and place them in a circle, approximately 2 inches (5 cm) from the center of the cake, and evenly spaced. Using a large, flat spatula, carefully center and place the 8-inch (20.5 cm) cake on top of the 9-inch (23 cm) cake. Make sure the top tier has a smooth icing finish before decorating.

5. Place the cake on a rotating cake turntable. Attach Wilton decorating tip #10 and the coupler to the pastry bag and fill with yellow buttercream frosting. Start at the bottom tier and create a row of dots by piping circles all along the bottom edge. When finished with the row around the entire cake, take an angled spatula and push down into the center of the dots to make scallops. Continue with the next row of dots, again circling the entire cake, pushing down on the dots to create another row of scallops. Finish the remainder of the cake until you reach the top edge. Repeat this process for the 8-inch (20.5 cm) top tier.

HAPPY CAMPERS CAKE TOPPER

I made a tiny tent topper from a scrap of fabric, five sticks, some twine and a glue gun. Using a plastic chocolate mold, I formed a chocolate sign and piped "Happy Trails" in buttercream.

Acorn Donuts

THESE SWEET ACORNS COULDN'T BE EASIER TO MAKE. JUST GRAB A BOX OF DONUT HOLES FROM YOUR LOCAL GROCERY STORE BAKERY, DIP IN CHOCOLATE, SPRINKLE AND ADD A PRETZEL TOP.

MAKES ABOUT 20 ACORNS

INGREDIENTS

STORE-BOUGHT DONUT HOLES (ABOUT 20)

1 (12-OUNCE [340 G]) PACKAGE CHOCOLATE CANDY MELTS

BROWN SPRINKLES

SMALL END PIECES OF PRETZEL STICKS

WAXED PAPER

DIRECTIONS

1. Melt the chocolate candy melts in a microwave-safe bowl in 30-second increments at 40% power for about 1½ minutes, stirring as needed until smooth.

2. Place brown sprinkles in a bowl.

3. Dip the top one-third of the donut holes in the melted chocolate candy, then dip into the brown sprinkles.

4. Insert a pretzel piece into each of the chocolate-dipped ends for the stems. Let dry on waxed paper.

Campground Cookies

I HAVE TO ADMIT THAT THIS IS MY HUSBAND'S SECRET COOKIE RECIPE. I CAN ALWAYS TELL HE'S TRYING TO GET ON MY GOOD SIDE WHEN I SMELL THESE COOKIES BAKING FROM THE KITCHEN. THESE HOMEMADE BUTTERY CHOCOLATE CHIP COOKIES ARE SO DELICIOUS, I CAN NEVER EAT JUST ONE (OR STAY UPSET).

MAKES 48 SMALL COOKIES

INGREDIENTS

4½ CUPS (281 G) ALL-PURPOSE FLOUR

2 TEASPOONS BAKING SODA

1½ TEASPOONS ALUMINUM-FREE BAKING POWDER

1 TEASPOON SALT

1½ CUPS (340 G) SALTED BUTTER, AT ROOM TEMPERATURE (3 STICKS)

1½ CUPS (300 G) GRANULATED SUGAR

1½ CUPS (340 G) PACKED LIGHT BROWN SUGAR

2 LARGE EGGS

2 TEASPOON PURE VANILLA EXTRACT

2 CUPS (160 G) WHOLE OATS

2 CUPS (360 G) MINI CHOCOLATE CHIPS

YOU WILL NEED

2 NONSTICK COOKIE SHEETS

SMALL COOKIE SCOOP

TWINE, JUTE OR RIBBON

DIRECTIONS

1. Preheat the oven to 375F (190°C).

2. In a large bowl, combine the flour, baking soda, baking powder and salt with a whisk. Set aside.

3. In a large mixing bowl, and using an electric mixer on medium speed with the paddle attachment, or with a large bowl and mixing spoon, beat the butter, granulated sugar and brown sugar until creamy, scraping the bowl with a rubber spatula as needed. Add the eggs and vanilla, and beat again until light and fluffy or until the batter is nice and smooth.

4. Turn the mixer speed to low, add half dry ingredients to the batter, and mix to combine. Add the remaining dry ingredients, and mix until the dough is smooth, scraping the bowl as needed.

5. Add the oats and mini chocolate chips, and mix only enough to combine.

6. Drop cookie dough by rounded tablespoons or cookie scoop onto ungreased cookie sheets, leaving enough room for cookies to spread, about 2 inches (5 cm) apart.

7. Bake the cookies for 7 to 10 minutes, or until light brown (centers will be soft). The cookies will continue to bake for a few minutes after they are removed from the oven. Let cool on the cookie sheet for 5 minutes before moving to wire racks.

8. Stack the cookies and tie with baker's twine, jute or ribbon.

Don't Feed the Bears Brownie Pops

THESE RICH BROWNIE POPS ARE THE PERFECT SIZE FOR FULFILLING A SWEET CRAVING.
DIP YOUR POPS IN RED CANDY MELTS AND TOP WITH RED SPRINKLES.

MAKES 25 POPS

INGREDIENTS

2 STANDARD-SIZE PACKAGES
BROWNIE MIX PLUS INDGEDIENTS ON
PACKAGE

½ TO ¾ CUP (120 TO 175 ML)
CHOCOLATE BUTTERCREAM (PAGE 10)

3 (12-OUNCE [340 G]) PACKAGES RED
CANDY MELTS

RED CANDY OIL

RED SPRINKLES

YOU WILL NEED

9 × 13-INCH (23 × 33 CM) BAKING PAN
OR CASSEROLE DISH

CLEAN STICKS OR BRANCHES FOR
LOLLIPOP STICKS

STYROFOAM

DIRECTIONS

1. Preheat the oven to 350°F (180°C). Lightly oil or spray the 9 × 13-inch (23 × 33 cm) baking pan with vegetable spray.

2. Make the brownie batter according to directions on the package. Spread the batter into the prepared baking pan.

3. Bake for 40 to 50 minutes (or follow the package directions), or until a toothpick inserted into the center comes out clean. Remove the pan from the oven and place on a wire cooling rack. Let cool completely.

4. Mash up the brownies and place in a large bowl. Using an electric stand mixer fitted with a paddle attachment, mix brownies and ½ to ¾ cup (120-175 ml) frosting on medium speed until well blended and mixture can be molded into a ball.

5. Measure and roll the mixture into tablespoon-size balls, place on a cookie sheet and refrigerate for 1 hour or until firm.

6. Melt candy melts in a microwave-safe bowl in 30-second increments, for about 1½ minutes at 40% power, stirring as needed until smooth.

7. Remove the brownie balls from refrigerator. Dip each stick or branch ¼ inch (6 mm) into melted candy, and then insert into each brownie ball. Place red sprinkles in a shallow bowl. Dip the pops in the melted candy and sprinkle red sprinkles to completely cover.

8. Stand in Styrofoam to dry.

Happy Trails Mix

THE HAPPY TRAILS MIX IS SO QUICK AND EASY, YOU'LL WONDER WHY IT'S EVEN A RECIPE.
IT'S SO SIMPLE TO THROW TOGETHER—THE PERFECT SNACK FOR A CAMPOUT.

MAKES 10 CUPS

INGREDIENTS

3 CUPS (85 G) CHEERIOS CEREAL

1 CUP (225 G) RED M&M'S

1 CUP HERSHEY'S DROPS

2 CUPS (390 G) WHOLE ALMONDS

2 CUPS (290 G) SALTED PEANUTS

2 CUPS (115 G) MINI MARSHMALLOWS

DIRECTIONS

Mix all the ingredients in a large bowl. Fill cups with equal portions. Serve in a large bowl or individual camping mugs.

Kumbaya Cupcakes

BURIED DEEP INSIDE THESE ULTRAMOIST DEVIL'S FOOD CHOCOLATE CUPCAKES, YOU'LL FIND EVERY KIDS' FAVORITE CANDY BAR—KIT KATS. THIS BATCH MAKES AN EQUAL NUMBER OF STANDARD SIZE CUPCAKES AND MINI CUPCAKES FOR ALL THE PAPA BEARS, MAMA BEARS AND THE CUTE LITTLE BABY BEARS. CHANGE THE BUTTERCREAM COLOR TO GO WITH YOUR CAMPING THEME.

MAKES 18 LARGE AND 18 MINI CUPCAKES

INGREDIENTS

1 (18.25-OUNCE [517 G]) BOX DUNCAN HINES DEVIL'S FOOD CAKE MIX

1 (3.4-OUNCE [110 G]) BOX JELL-O CHOCOLATE INSTANT PUDDING AND PIE FILLING, DRY

1 CUP (235 ML) WATER

⅓ CUP (80 ML) VEGETABLE OIL

4 LARGE EGGS

2 BATCHES BUTTERCREAM FROSTING (PAGE 10)

BLUE AMERICOLOR BRIGHT BLUE SOFT GEL PASTE COLOR

36 RED M&M'S

KIT KAT BITES, CHOPPED INTO SMALL SQUARES

YOU WILL NEED

2 STANDARD, AND 2 MINI CUPCAKE TRAYS

18 STANDARD, AND 18 MINI PAPER CUPCAKE LINERS

COOKIE SCOOP

1 LARGE PASTRY BAG

#869 ATECO DECORATING TIP

DIRECTIONS

1. Preheat the oven to 350°F (180°C). Line the cupcake trays with paper cupcake liners. Set the prepared trays aside.

2. In a large bowl, and using an electric stand mixer fitted with a paddle attachment, beat the cake mix, pudding mix, water, oil and eggs on medium speed for 2 to 3 minutes, or until well blended. Scrape down the sides of the bowl, and mix again until all the ingredients are incorporated.

3. Using a cookie scoop, place some cake batter (filling about one-third full) into each paper liner, add a few Kit Kat bites, and top with more batter to fill the liner (about two-thirds full total), dividing evenly between the cupcake trays.

4. Bake the large cupcakes for 18 to 20 minutes, and the mini cupcakes for 10 to 13 minutes, or until a toothpick inserted into the center comes out clean. Remove the cupcakes from the oven and place the trays on wire cooling racks for 15 minutes. Take the cupcakes out of the trays and allow them to cool completely on the wire racks before decorating.

5. Place the #869 Ateco decorating tip inside the pastry bag (no need to use a coupler) and fill with blue frosting.

6. Starting from the edge of the cupcake, begin to squeeze decorating bag using consistent pressure, and in a clockwise motion, swirl around a few times until you get to the top. Decorate the top with a red M&M.

Great Outdoors S'mores

WHETHER YOUR TENT IS PITCHED AT A CAMPGROUND OR IN YOUR OWN BACKYARD, NO CAMPING TRIP IS COMPLETE WITHOUT S'MORES. MAKE THESE SPECIAL BY USING HALF HERSHEY'S ALMOND BARS, AND HALF COOKIES N' CREAM BARS—AND EXTRA BIG BY USING JUMBO MARSHMALLOWS. TIE THEM UP WITH COLORFUL RIBBONS.

MAKES 12 S'MORES

INGREDIENTS

1 BOX GRAHAM CRACKERS (12 GRAHAM CRACKER SHEETS BROKEN IN HALF)

3 REGULAR-SIZE HERSHEY'S ALMOND BARS

3 REGULAR-SIZE HERSHEY'S COOKIES N' CREME BARS

12 JUMBO MARSHMALLOWS

YOU WILL NEED

COOKIE SHEET

TWINE OR RIBBON

DIRECTIONS

1. Break the graham crackers and Hershey bars in half. Place half the graham crackers on the cookie sheet.

2. Layer half the crackers with one half piece of the Hershey's Cookies 'n' Creme Bars, and the remaining halves with Hershey's Almond Bars.

3. Top each with one marshmallow laid sideways, then with the remaining graham cracker halves.

4. Tie up the s'mores with twine or ribbon.

S'mores on a Stick

MAKES 18 S'MORES

INGREDIENTS

18 JUMBO MARSHMALLOWS

GRAHAM CRACKER CRUMBS

1 (12-OUNCE [280 G]) PACKAGE CHOCOLATE CANDY MELTS

YOU WILL NEED

18 TREE BRANCHES, OR STICKS

STYROFOAM

DIRECTIONS

1. Insert the sticks into the marshmallows and set aside.

2. Melt chocolate candy melts in a microwave-safe bowl in 30-second increments at 40% power for about 1½ minutes, stirring as needed until smooth.

3. Dip the marshmallows halfway into the melted chocolate. They don't have to be perfect. A little drippy looks just as great.

4. Sprinkle the graham cracker crumbs on top, making sure to let a layer of chocolate show.

5. Stand the S'mores Sticks in Styrofoam to dry.

Campout Jenny Cookies

THE CAMPOUT DESSERT TABLE OVERFLOWS WITH FUN, COLORFUL DESSERTS. BUT MY FAVORITES ARE THE CAMP-THEMED SUGAR COOKIES. IF YOU WISH TO MAKE ALL FIVE SUGAR COOKIES ON THE CAMPOUT DESSERT TABLE AS THEY'RE PICTURED, MAKE ONE BATCH OF BUTTERCREAM FROSTING AS DIRECTED ON PAGE 10 AND TINT EACH WITH THE APPROPRIATE COLORS.

ATTACH WILTON DECORATING TIPS AND COUPLERS TO EACH OF THE PASTRY BAGS AND FILL WITH FROSTING; ONE EACH WITH WHITE FROSTING, BROWN, BLUE, IVORY AND DARK RED (MADE BY ADDING A DROP OF BROWN COLORING TO RED FROSTING). YOU'LL BE MAKING JUST ONE BATCH OF SUGAR COOKIE DOUGH AND USING IT FOR ALL FIVE COOKIE SHAPES. IT'S EASIER TO DECORATE THE COOKIES WITH THE WHITE FROSTING FIRST, THEN TINT THE REMAINING FROSTING WITH THE COLORS NEEDED. SEE PAGE 12 FOR THE COOKIE INGREDIENTS AND DIRECTIONS.

MAKES ABOUT 24 COOKIES

YOU WILL NEED

ROLLING PIN
2 NONSTICK COOKIE SHEETS
COOKIE SPATULA
CANOE COOKIE CUTTER
TEPEE TENT COOKIE CUTTER
MOOSE HEAD COOKIE CUTTER
SQUIRREL COOKIE CUTTER
PINECONE COOKIE CUTTER
4 DISPOSABLE PASTRY BAGS
4 #4 WILTON DECORATING TIPS
4 #18 WILTON DECORATING TIPS
4 WILTON COUPLERS
AMERICOLOR SOFT GEL PASTE COLORS TO MAKE BROWN, BLUE, DARK RED, IVORY
BROWN SPRINKLES
BROWN SANDING SUGAR

Pinecone Cookies

INGREDIENTS

BROWN BUTTERCREAM

To decorate the pinecone cookies, place brown buttercream frosting in a pastry bag fitted with a #18 Wilton decorating tip. Beginning at the top of the cookie, and squeezing the bag with gentle pressure, lift it up a bit and then down again to touch the cookie to resemble scales on a pinecone. Using the same technique, repeat consecutive rows across the cookie, adding extra swirls of frosting scales toward the middle and less as you reach the bottom of the cookie. Add a little frosting stem at the very bottom of the pinecone.

(continued)

Teepee Tent Cookies

INGREDIENTS

IVORY BUTTERCREAM

BROWN BUTTERCREAM

BLUE BUTTERCREAM

DARK RED BUTTERCREAM

To decorate the teepee tent cookies, place the ivory buttercream frosting in a pastry bag fitted with a #4 Wilton decorating tip. Begin by outlining teepee, stopping just before reaching the top. Fill in the outline with the frosting, running it horizontally from one edge of the outline to the other, until completely filled in. Use dark red frosting and a #4 tip to draw two lines near the bottom. Use blue frosting and a #4 tip to draw a zigzag near the top. Add two teepee poles at the very top using brown frosting and a #4 tip.

Moose Head Cookies

INGREDIENTS

BROWN BUTTERCREAM

BLACK BUTTERCREAM

BROWN SANDING SUGAR

To decorate the moose head cookies, place the brown buttercream frosting in a pastry bag fitted with a #4 Wilton decorating tip. Begin by outlining both the moose's antlers first. Fill in the antlers with frosting, then turn upside down in the brown sanding sugar to adhere and coat the antlers completely. Fill in the moose outline with the frosting, running it horizontally from one edge of the outline to the other, until both the head is filled in. Using a pastry bag with black frosting, and fitted with a #4 Wilton decorating tip, give the moose two eyes.

Squirrel Cookies

INGREDIENTS

BROWN BUTTERCREAM

BLACK BUTTERCREAM

BROWN SPRINKLES

To decorate the squirrel cookies, place the brown buttercream frosting in a pastry bag fitted with a #4 Wilton decorating tip. Begin by outlining the tail of the squirrel first, then turn upside down in the brown sprinkles to adhere and cover the tail completely. Outline the rest of the squirrel, and fill in with brown frosting, running it horizontally from one edge of the outlines to the other, until the body is filled in. Using a pastry bag with black frosting, and fitted with a #4 Wilton decorating tip, give the squirrel an eye and a nose.

Canoe Cookies

INGREDIENTS

RED BUTTERCREAM WITH BROWN COLORING

BROWN BUTTERCREAM

BLUE BUTTERCREAM

In a small bowl, mix one drop of brown coloring into a small amount (about 1 cup) of red frosting to make dark red. To decorate the canoe cookies, place the buttercream frosting in a pastry bag fitted with a #4 Wilton decorating tip. Outline the canoe, then fill in the outline with the dark red frosting running it vertically from one edge of the outline to the other, until the canoe is filled in. Use brown frosting to add a canoe oar. Use blue frosting and a #4 tip to add a different registration number to each canoe in the upper right corner.

10

Fall Bounty

GROWING UP IN THE PACIFIC NORTHWEST, I'VE BEEN BLESSED TO EXPERIENCE ALL FOUR SEASONS—FROM COLD BLUSTERY WINTERS TO VERY RAINY SPRINGS, BEAUTIFUL SUMMERS, AND MY FAVORITE SEASON OF ALL, FALL. IN FALL, SEATTLE IS ONE OF THE MOST GORGEOUS PLACES TO BE. THE TREES ARE FILLED WITH FIERY RED, VIBRANT YELLOW AND DEEP, RICH GOLD LEAVES. THE PANORAMIC VIEWS OF THE MOUNTAINS AND HILLSIDES ARE BREATHTAKING. WE GET TO COZY UP IN WARM FALL CLOTHES WHILE SIPPING PUMPKIN SPICE LATTES AND NIBBLING ON PUMPKIN-SHAPED SUGAR COOKIES.

FOR ME, FALL IS JUST THE BEGINNING OF BAKING SEASON. IT'S LIKE A PRACTICE ROUND, AN INTRODUCTION LEADING UP TO THE BIG CHRISTMAS SEASON. STORES BEGIN DISPLAYING THEIR CANNED PUMPKIN PUREES, BAKING SPICES, PIE FILLINGS AND FALL COOKIE CUTTERS. JUST SEEING THE DISPLAYS AT THE HEADS OF THE AISLES GET ME EXCITED—IT'S TIME TO GET BAKING.

It's also the perfect season for dessert tables. You can fill them with pumpkin-shaped sugar cookies, mini apple pies and pumpkin spice cake pops, just to name a few. Kids and adults alike enjoy a caramel apple, no matter how long it takes to pick the caramel out of your teeth.

One of our family's fall traditions is spending an afternoon at our favorite pumpkin patch. The owners are sweet as can be and have run the family farm for generations. The entrance overflows with colored pumpkins, gourds and lovely fall plants. The display is always so beautiful, I can't help but imagine filling it in with desserts. The owners laugh because I'm always complimenting them on their amazing old wooden tables and metal display shelves. They say, "It's so old"! I say, "That's what I love!!" The weathered wood, the rusty metal and the bounty of pumpkins make such a stunning combination—it's a huge source of inspiration.

SETTING THE TABLE

You can build your table using worn wooden boxes and benches. The benches and boxes establish height on the table, a key element in the design. Try adding colored pumpkins, gourds and tins with fall flowers for added pops of color. Desserts can be set atop vintage amber-colored glass and old cast-iron pans turned upside down. I found an old red metal box and black enamelware tray for cookies and a rusty round tin that made the perfect cake plate. Instead of using a tray or platter for the caramel apples, I utilized the wooden cabinet shelves for display, and placed the pumpkin cake pops inside a small wooden drawer topped with hay. The assortment of random display pieces combined with the textures, fall colors and sweet pumpkin-scented desserts are sure to put your guests in an autumn mood.

FALL BOUNTY DESSERTS

- ♥ **German Chocolate Harvest Cake**
- ♥ **Pumpkin Patch Cake Pops**
- ♥ **Rice Krispie Treat Pumpkins**
- ♥ **Nutty Caramel Apples**
- ♥ **Autumn Apple Pies**
- ♥ **Pumpkin Spice Sandwich Cookies**
- ♥ **Scarecrow Cookies**
- ♥ **Wheelbarrow Cookies**
- ♥ **Fall Leaf Cookies**
- ♥ **Pumpkin Cookies**
- ♥ **Owl Cookies**

German Chocolate Harvest Cake

**THIS GERMAN CHOCOLATE CAKE IS ONE OF MY FAVORITES.
ITS UNIQUE TEXTURE IS ALWAYS A CONVERSATION PIECE.**

*Note: This cake is large and uses three boxes of standard cake mix. The bowl of a standard electric stand mixer is not large enough
to hold ingredients for such a large amount. You may have to mix the batter and bake the cake in two or more batches.*

MAKES ONE 6-INCH (15 CM) AND 8-INCH (20.5 CM) TIERED CAKE

INGREDIENTS

COOKING SPRAY OR CRISCO OR
BUTTER PLUS FLOUR, FOR PANS

3 (18.25-OUNCE OUNCE [517 G]) BOXES
DUNCAN HINES GERMAN CHOCOLATE
CAKE MIX

3 (3.4-OUNCE [110 G]) BOXES JELL-O
CHOCOLATE INSTANT PUDDING AND
PIE FILLING, DRY

3 CUPS (710 ML) WATER

1 CUP (235 ML) OIL

12 LARGE EGGS

2 CANS PECAN COCONUT ICING

3 BATCHES BUTTERCREAM FROSTING
(PAGE 10)

1½ CUPS (150 G) PECANS, CHOPPED

DIRECTIONS

1. Preheat the oven to 350°F (180°C). Coat the 6-inch (15 cm) and 8-inch (20.5 cm) round nonstick cake pans with cooking spray or grease and flour the pans, tapping out the excess flour. Set the prepared pans aside.

2. In a large bowl, and using an electric stand mixer fitted with a paddle attachment, beat the cake mix, pudding mix, water, oil and eggs on medium speed for 2 to 3 minutes, or until well blended. Scrape the sides of the bowl and mix again until all the ingredients are incorporated.

3. Pour batter into the prepared cake pans, filling each one approximately three-quarters full.

4. Place the pans in the preheated oven, on the middle rack. Bake the 6-inch (15 cm) cakes for 25 to 30 minutes, and the 8-inch (20.5 cm) cakes for 30 to 35 minutes, or until a toothpick inserted into the center comes out clean. Depending on your oven size, cakes may need to bake in seperate batches.

5. Remove the pans from the oven and place on wire cooling racks for 25 to 30 minutes. Run a knife around the edges of the cakes, flip the pans over, and gently extract the cakes. Return the cakes to the wire racks and finish cooling completely before frosting and decorating. After the layers are cooled, freeze or refrigerate the cakes for 1 hour before decorating to reduce crumbs and make for a smoother icing process.

6. Meanwhile, make the three batches of buttercream frosting. Add one can of pecan coconut frosting, and beat until well blended.

(continued)

3 (8 × 2-INCH [10.5 × 5 CM]) AND
2 (6 × 2-INCH [15 × 5 CM]) ROUND
NONSTICK CAKE PANS

CAKE CUTTER OR LONG, SERRATED
KNIFE

2 ROUND CARDBOARD OR PLASTIC
CAKE BOARDS

OFFSET ANGLED SPATULA

5 (¼-INCH [6 MM]-THICK) DOWELS OR
THICK PLASTIC STRAWS

LARGE, FLAT SPATULA

CAKE DECORATING TURNTABLE

LARGE DECORATING SPATULA

CAKE SCRAPER

TO ASSEMBLE AND DECORATE THE CAKE

1. Before decorating, trim the crowns from the cake tops with a cake cutter or long, serrated knife so they are flat and even.

2. Place one of the 8-inch (20.5 cm) cakes on a cake board cut side up. Using the angled cake spatula, spread ½ can of pecan coconut icing evenly across the top of the first cake layer.

3. Place the second and third 8-inch (20.5 cm) cakes on top of the first, with cut sides on the bottom, and filling with another ½ cup (120 ml) of pecan coconut icing between each layer.

4. Use the angled cake spatula to cover the cake completely with a very thin layer of buttercream frosting (or crumb coat) to help reduce the amount of crumbs in the final coat of icing. Set the two-tiered 8-inch (20.5 cm) cake aside.

5. Repeat this process with the 6-inch (15 cm) cake layers, using the remaining ½ cup (120 ml) of pecan coconut icing between the layers, and icing the top and sides of the cake with the buttercream frosting. Once the same process has been completed on the 6-inch (15 cm) cake layers, allow them to dry for 1 hour, or until the icing crusts.

6. Create supports for the smaller cake to sit atop the larger cake by placing the dowels into the top of the 8-inch (20.5 cm) cake. Insert the first dowel into the cake and use a pen to mark the dowel at the point where it just comes to the top of the cake. Remove the dowel and cut it at that mark. Cut three to four additional dowels or straws to the same length and place them in a circle, approximately 2 inches (5 cm) from the center of the cake, and evenly spaced. Using a large, flat spatula, carefully center and place the 6-inch (15 cm) cake on top of the 8-inch (20.5 cm) cake.

7. Place the cake on a rotating cake turntable. Starting at the top of the cake, and using a large decorating spatula, frost the top of the cake. Continue with the sides of both tiers, icing it with a rough spackled finish (as shown in photo). Finish icing the remainder of the cake until you reach the bottom. Pat chopped nuts along the bottom for 2 to 2½ inches (5 to 6.5 cm).

Pumpkin Patch Cake Pops

KIDS LOVE THESE FUN PUMPKIN-SHAPED CAKE POPS AS MUCH AS ADULTS LOVE THE PUMPKIN-SPICE FLAVOR HIDDEN INSIDE.

MAKES 40 CAKE POPS

INGREDIENTS

1 (18.25-OUNCE [517 G]) BOX DUNCAN HINES SPICE CAKE MIX

1 CUP (245 G) PURE PUMPKIN PUREE (NOT PUMPKIN PIE FILLING)

¾ CUP (175 ML) WATER

⅓ CUP (80 ML) OIL

4 LARGE EGGS

1 (16-OUNCE [454 G]) CAN DUNCAN HINES CREAMY HOME-STYLE CREAM CHEESE FROSTING

3 (12-OUNCE [340 G]) PACKAGES ORANGE CANDY MELTS

1 CUP (208 G) GREEN CANDY MELTS

PRETZEL STICKS

YOU WILL NEED

9 × 13-INCH (23 × 33 CM) BAKING PAN OR CASSEROLE DISH

40 (5-INCH [7.5 CM]) LOLLIPOP STICKS

STYROFOAM

DISPOSABLE PASTRY BAG

DIRECTIONS

1. Preheat the oven to 350°F (180°C). Coat the 9 × 13-inch (23 × 33 cm) baking pan with cooking spray, or grease and flour the pan, tapping out the excess flour. Set aside.

2. In a large bowl, and using an electric stand mixer fitted with a paddle attachment, beat the cake mix, pumpkin puree, water, oil and eggs on medium speed for 2 to 3 minutes, or until well blended. Scrape the sides of the bowl and mix again until all the ingredients are incorporated.

3. Pour the batter into the prepared cake pan. Place the pan in the preheated oven, and bake for 35 to 40 minutes, or until a toothpick inserted into the center comes out clean.

4. Remove the pan from the oven and place on a wire cooling rack for 25 to 30 minutes. Let cool completely before making the cake pops.

5. Mash up the cake and place in a large bowl. Using an electric stand mixer fitted with a paddle attachment, mix the cake and ½ to ¾ cup (120 to 175 ml) of the cream cheese frosting on medium speed until moist and well blended and the mixture can be molded into a ball.

6. Measure and roll the mixture into 1 tablespoon-size balls and place on a cookie sheet. Refrigerate for 1 hour, or until firm.

7. Melt the candy melts in separate microwave-safe bowls in 30-second increments at 40% power for about 2 to 3 minutes, stirring as needed until smooth.

8. Remove the pops from the refrigerator. Dip each lollipop stick ¼ inch (6 mm) into the melted candy. Insert the sticks into all the cake balls. (The melted candy will adhere the lollipop sticks to the cake balls to prevent them from falling off the sticks when dipping).

9. Proceed to dip entire cake balls down into the melted candy. Insert a very small piece of pretzel into the top of the pumpkin pops. Stand up the pops in a sheet of Styrofoam to dry.

10. Pour the melted green candy into the disposable pastry bag. Cut off the tip with scissors to make a small hole. Draw a squiggly pumpkin vine on each pumpkin. Return to the Styrofoam to dry.

Rice Krispie Treat Pumpkins

YOU CAN'T HELP BUT LOVE THESE ADORABLE LITTLE PUMPKINS MOLDED FROM
RICE KRISPIE BATTER. FOR EXTRA CREDIT, DRAW ON A JACK-O'-LANTERN FACE
WITH THE MELTED BLACK CANDY MELTS.

MAKES 24 TREATS

INGREDIENTS

3 TABLESPOONS (42 G) BUTTER OR
MARGARINE

1 (10-OUNCE [280 G]) PACKAGE MINI
MARSHMALLOWS (4 CUPS)

AMERICOLOR ORANGE SOFT GEL PASTE
COLOR

6 CUPS (150 G) RICE KRISPIES CEREAL

12 MINI TOOTSIE ROLLS, CUT IN HALF

YOU WILL NEED

COOKIE SCOOP

WAXED PAPER

DIRECTIONS

1. In a large saucepan over low heat, melt the butter. Add the marshmallows and stir until melted and smooth. Remove the pan from the heat. Add the orange food coloring and stir again.

2. Add the Rice Krispies and stir until completely coated. Let cool (about 2 minutes) until the mixture can be handled safely.

3. Using a cookie scoop, measure and scoop the Rice Krispie mixture into uniform balls. Spray your hands with nonstick cooking spray (Pam or Crisco), and finish rolling the mixture into balls by hand. Place on waxed paper.

4. To decorate, stick a piece of Tootsie Roll into the top of each pumpkin.

Nutty Caramel Apples

THIS IS A FANTASTIC FALL COMBO: CRISP, JUICY APPLES MIXED WITH NUTTY CARAMEL. CUSTOMIZE THESE TREATS BY EXCHANGING THE NUTS FOR MINI M&M'S, COCONUT FLAKES, RAINBOW SPRINKLES OR EVEN DRIZZLE THEM WITH ANOTHER FLAVOR OF CHOCOLATE.

MAKES 12 APPLES

INGREDIENTS

12 APPLES

BUTTER, FOR PAN

2 (9-OUNCE [225 G]) BAGS CARAMELS, UNWRAPPED

4 TABLESPOONS (60 ML) WHOLE MILK

2 CUPS (200 G) WALNUTS, CHOPPED

2 (12-OUNCE [340 G]) PACKAGE CHOCOLATE CANDY MELTS

YOU WILL NEED

12 WOODEN CRAFT OR POPSICLE STICKS

WAXED PAPER

JUTE OR TWINE

DIRECTIONS

1. Lightly butter a baking sheet and set aside.

2. Remove the stems and stick a wooden craft stick into the top of each apple.

3. Melt the caramel and milk in a microwave-safe bowl in 30-second increments at 40% power for about 1½ minutes, stirring once as needed until smooth. Cool slightly for about 2 minutes.

4. Quickly dip and roll the apples in the caramel sauce until completely coated. Place on the prepared baking sheet until dry.

5. Melt the chocolate candy melts in a microwave-safe bowl in 30-second increments at 40% power for about 1½ minutes, stirring as needed until smooth.

6. Dip the caramel apples in the melted chocolate about half way, then roll in the chopped nuts. Place on waxed paper. Tie the sticks with jute or twine bows.

Autumn Apple Pies

IT WOULDN'T BE FALL WITHOUT AN APPLE PIE. THESE CLASSIC PIES MADE MINIATURE CAPTURE THE FLAVOR AND ESSENCE OF FALL. CUT A VENTING HOLE IN YOUR PIE TOP WITH A MINI FALL COOKIE CUTTER SHAPED AS AN APPLE, PUMPKIN, LEAF OR ALL THREE! FINISH BY ATTACHING A WOODEN SPOON WITH JUTE.

MAKES 12 APPLE PIES

INGREDIENTS

2 STANDARD-SIZE BOXES PILLSBURY PIE CRUST

FLOUR, FOR ROLLING

2 (21-OUNCE [595 G]) CANS APPLE PIE FILLING, CUT UP INTO SMALL CHUNKS

YOU WILL NEED

ROLLING PIN

STANDARD-SIZE MUFFIN TRAY

LARGE ROUND COOKIE CUTTER

MINIATURE LEAF COOKIE CUTTER

WOODEN SPOONS

TWINE

DIRECTIONS

1. Preheat the oven to 425°F (220°C).

2. Remove the crust from the pouch and roll out on a lightly floured surface. Using the large round cookie cutter, cut out circles, gathering up pie crusts scraps and rerolling to make a total of twenty-four pie crust circles. Press twelve pie crust rounds into ungreased muffin cups.

3. Spoon about 1½ tablespoons of the chopped apple pie filling into each pie crust.

4. Using the leaf cookie cutter, cut shapes out of the remaining twelve pie crust circles. Place on the apple pies and crimp or pinch tops, sealing the edges.

5. Bake the pies for 18 to 20 minutes, or until the crusts are golden brown. Let cool completely in the pan before removing, about 30 minutes.

6. Using a sharp knife, loosen the edges and gently remove the mini pies from the muffin cups.

7. Tie wooden spoons onto each pie with twine.

Pumpkin Spice Sandwich Cookies

THESE COOKIES HAVE ALL THE SWEETNESS AND SPICES THAT YOU'D FIND IN GRANDMA'S PUMPKIN PIE. CAKEY PUMPKIN COOKIES SANDWICHED TOGETHER WITH MY FAVORITE BUTTERCREAM ICING; THEY'RE THE PERFECT TREAT FOR A CRISP FALL DAY.

MAKES 18 SANDWICH COOKIES

INGREDIENTS

2 CUPS (250 G) ALL-PURPOSE FLOUR

1 TEASPOON BAKING SODA

1 TEASPOON PUMPKIN PIE SPICE

½ TEASPOON ALUMINUM-FREE BAKING POWDER

½ TEASPOON SALT

½ CUP (112 G) BUTTER (1 STICK), AT ROOM TEMPERATURE

1 CUP (225 G) FIRMLY PACKED BROWN SUGAR

1 LARGE EGG

½ CUP (12.5 G) PURE PUMPKIN PUREE (NOT PUMPKIN PIE FILLING)

¼ CUP (60 ML) WHOLE MILK

1 TEASPOON PURE VANILLA EXTRACT

3 CUPS (710 ML) BUTTERCREAM FROSTING (PAGE 10)

YOU WILL NEED

2 NONSTICK COOKIE SHEETS

MINI COOKIE SCOOP

DISPOSABLE PASTRY BAG

DIRECTIONS

1. Preheat the oven to 350°F (180°C).

2. In a large bowl, combine the flour, baking soda, pumpkin pie spice, baking powder and salt with a whisk. Set aside.

3. In a large mixing bowl, and using an electric mixer on medium speed with the paddle attachment, or with a large bowl and mixing spoon, beat the butter and brown sugar until creamy. Add the egg, pumpkin, milk and vanilla, and beat again until light and fluffy, or until the batter is nice and smooth, scraping the bowl with a rubber spatula as needed.

4. Turn the mixer speed to low, add half of the dry ingredients to the batter, and mix to combine. Add the remaining dry ingredients, and mix until the dough is smooth, scraping the bowl as needed.

5. Drop the cookie dough, using a mini cookie scoop or by rounded teaspoons, onto ungreased cookie sheets, leaving enough room for the cookies to spread.

6. Bake the cookies 7 to 8 minutes, or until set and lightly browned around the edges. Let cool on the cookie sheet for 2 minutes before moving to wire racks. Let cool completely.

7. Turn half of the cookies upside down on a cookie sheet. Using a pastry bag or knife, fill half of the cookies with buttercream frosting. Top with the remaining cookies to make sandwiches.

Fall Bounty Jenny Cookies

CELEBRATE THE CHANGE IN SEASONS WITH THESE ADORABLE FALL THEMED SUGAR COOKIES. PACKAGE THEM IN CELLOPHANE BAGS TIED WITH JUTE OR RAFFIA FOR YOUR CHILDREN'S TEACHERS FOR A FESTIVE TREAT.

IF YOU WISH TO MAKE ALL FIVE SUGAR COOKIES ON THE FALL TABLE AS THEY'RE PICTURED, MAKE ONE BATCH OF BUTTERCREAM FROSTING AS DIRECTED ON PAGE 10, DIVIDE AND TINT EACH WITH THE APPROPRIATE COLORS; ONE WITH WHITE FROSTING, BROWN, ORANGE, YELLOW AND GREEN. ATTACH WILTON DECORATING TIPS AND COUPLERS TO EACH OF THE PASTRY BAGS AND FILL WITH FROSTING. IT'S EASIER TO TINT THE FROSTING AND FILL THE BAGS AHEAD OF TIME. ALL FIVE COLORS USE #4 WILTON TIPS, AND ONE #104 TIP. YOU'LL BE MAKING JUST ONE BATCH OF SUGAR COOKIE DOUGH, AND USING IT FOR ALL FIVE COOKIE SHAPES. SEE PAGE 12 FOR THE COOKIE INGREDIENTS AND DIRECTIONS.

MAKES ABOUT 24 COOKIES

YOU WILL NEED

ROLLING PIN
2 NONSTICK COOKIE SHEETS
COOKIE SPATULA
PUMPKIN COOKIE CUTTER
SCARECROW COOKIE CUTTER
WHEELBARROW COOKIE CUTTER
LARGE LEAF COOKIE CUTTER
OWL COOKIE CUTTER
5 DISPOSABLE PASTRY BAGS
5 #4 WILTON DECORATING TIPS
1 #104 WILTON DECORATING TIPS
5 WILTON COUPLERS
AMERICOLOR SOFT GEL PASTE COLORS
TO MAKE BROWN, ORANGE, GREEN,
YELLOW

Pumpkin Cookies

INGREDIENTS

ORANGE BUTTERCREAM
BROWN BUTTERCREAM

To decorate the pumpkin cookies, place orange the buttercream frosting in a pastry bag fitted with a #4 Wilton decorating tip. Begin by outlining the pumpkin. Fill in the outline with the frosting, running it vertically from one edge of the outline to the other, until the pumpkin is filled in. Using a pastry bag with brown frosting, and fitted with a #4 Wilton decorating tip, outline and fill in the pumpkin stem.

(continued)

Scarecrow Cookies

INGREDIENTS
ORANGE BUTTERCREAM
BROWN BUTTERCREAM
YELLOW BUTTERCREAM
GREEN BUTTERCREAM

To decorate the scarecrow cookies, use the pastry bag filled with orange frosting, and fitted with a #4 Wilton decorating tip, and begin by outlining the scarecrow's shirt. Fill in the outlines with orange frosting, running it horizontally from one edge of the outlines to the other, until the shirt is filled in. Using a pastry bag with brown frosting, and fitted with a #4 Wilton decorating tip, outline his pants and hat, then fill in the outlines with brown frosting running it horizontally until completely filled in. Using the pastry bag filled with yellow buttercream and a #4 decorating tip, give the scarecrow straw arms and legs, and draw a yellow patch on his pants. Use the green frosting to draw a belt around his middle.

Owl Cookies

INGREDIENTS
ORANGE BUTTERCREAM
YELLOW BUTTERCREAM
GREEN BUTTERCREAM
WHITE BUTTERCREAM

To decorate the owl cookies, place the brown buttercream frosting in a pastry bag fitted with a #4 Wilton decorating tip, and outline the entire owl. Fill in the owl's wings running the frosting horizontally. Fill in the owl's body using a #104 Wilton tip, and beginning at the bottom, make a row of ruffles following the owl's curves. Overlapping the first row, repeat with another two rows of ruffles. Continue to just under the owl's head, running the ruffles horizontally from one edge of the outline to the other. Fill in the owl's head running the lines horizontally. Make two white eyes with brown pupils, and add an orange beak.

Fall Leaf Cookies

INGREDIENTS
ORANGE BUTTERCREAM
YELLOW BUTTERCREAM
GREEN BUTTERCREAM

To decorate the fall leaf cookies, use separate pastry bags each filled with orange, yellow and green frosting, and each fitted with a #4 Wilton decorating tip. Begin by outlining each leaf cookie. Fill in the outlines with the same color frosting, running it horizontally from one edge of the outlines to the other, until the cookies are completely filled in.

Wheelbarrow Cookies

INGREDIENTS
ORANGE BUTTERCREAM
BROWN BUTTERCREAM
GREEN BUTTERCREAM
WHITE BUTTERCREAM

To decorate the wheelbarrow cookies, use the pastry bag filled with green frosting, and fitted with a #4 Wilton decorating tip, and outline the body of the wheelbarrow. Fill in the outline with green frosting, running it horizontally from one edge of the outlines to the other, until the wheelbarrow is filled in. Using a pastry bag with orange frosting, and fitted with a #4 Wilton decorating tip, make four to five round pumpkins on top of the wheelbarrow. Using the pastry bag filled with brown buttercream and a #4 decorating tip, draw a wheelbarrow handle and wheel, and complete the pumpkins with tiny brown stems. Using the pastry bag with white buttercream, fill the wheelbarrow wheel.

11

North Pole Bakery

AS YOU KNOW BY NOW, I'M A HUGE FAN OF VINTAGE. I LOVE THE MYSTERY OF THE STORIES BEHIND THE TREASURES I FIND. WHEN IT COMES TO ANTIQUE SHOPPING OR FLEA MARKETS, I'M DRAWN TO TWO THINGS: THE FIRST AND OBVIOUS BEING VINTAGE GLASS CAKE PLATES (WITH EIGHTY-FIVE RUBBERMAIDS STUFFED FULL OF THEM IN MY GARAGE, YOU'D THINK I'D STOP BUYING THEM), AND SECOND, ANYTHING VINTAGE CHRISTMAS. I LIVE FOR THE ORNAMENT BOXES FILLED WITH SHINY BRIGHT GLASS ORNAMENTS, THE ASSORTMENT OF SANTAS BIG AND SMALL, BOTTLEBRUSH TREES, SWEET NATIVITY SCENES AND MOST OF ALL, VINTAGE ELVES.

Our Elf on the Shelf is named Buddy. He sits in simple places like bookshelves, countertops and window sills—and increasingly creative locations. He went from hopping bookshelves to decorating miniature cookies, cake pops and cakes in our kitchen, to showing up in the kids' car seats buckled and ready for church. Three Christmases ago, Buddy showed up with a lady friend named Snowflake (a vintage white elf), someone to cause even more trouble with. They dressed up in Ally's Barbie clothes, sent candy grams to her classroom at school and decorated her wood dollhouse for Christmas. When they said good-bye on Christmas Eve, they filled our entire family frame wall with thirty pictures of themselves, in hopes we wouldn't forget them until the next Christmas. And my kids didn't. They could hardly wait for the elves to come back. The following year, they arrived the morning after Thanksgiving in a hot air balloon complete with helium balloons and a comfortable basket for their long journey down from the North Pole.

I'm all about creating traditions for my kids. I strive to make real moments that my children will grow up remembering. I want to raise Ally and Hudson with expectations and excitement for the next holiday season or family affair. Whether it's the excitement of waking up each morning the entire month of December searching for the elves, or counting on me to throw a gingerbread house decorating party for all their friends, I want their childhood to be filled with joy and magical memories.

It's not just in the insane elf tradition or crazy parties I throw. It's the little things. It's knowing that at the Keller (farm) house, it's not Christmas until we've made fudge and delivered a few batches to the gospel mission. It's the excitement of pulling out the Christmas decorations and oohing and aahing over each and every nostalgic ornament that's unwrapped, while Daddy hangs from the roof making sure each Christmas light is strung in a perfectly straight line. It's the anticipation of holding their very own candle at our church's Christmas Eve candlelight service and remembering the real reason we celebrate the Christmas season.

Within all of these reasons, I find so much joy in antiques and vintage pieces. They all have a story. The old-fashioned Christmas ornaments may have once belonged to a mother who also let her children joyfully unwrap them while decorating their home for Christmas. Maybe the faded and worn angel tree topper sat upon the Cleaver family's tree for generations. Old lighted Santas probably lit numerous porches and greeted guests with cheer. And I'm sure many mothers warned their children not to lose Baby Jesus from the Nativity scene.

The winter season means different things to different people, but one thing the universe can agree on is the plentitude of dessert the holiday season brings. While I was growing up, my grandma always made Christmas special with her crispy sugar cookies shaped as stars, angels and candy canes, iced by hand with a butter knife. Her sugar cookies were accompanied by her melt-in-your-mouth fudge and snowball cookies. Now I make fudge with my kids, roll the same doughy snowball cookies in powdered sugar, and bake Christmas-shaped sugar cookies. The sugar cookies I enjoyed as a child have since been replaced with my mother-in-law's soft cookie recipe, making it even more special, passed down by both great-grandma and grandma to Ally and Hudson.

I wanted my Christmas dessert table to represent things my family enjoys traditionally during the holiday season with new twists and flavors. I kept Grandma's powdery snowball cookies classic but topped her signature fudge with crushed candy canes. I shaped my cookies as reindeer, angels, snowflakes, Santa hats and snowmen. I topped the holiday cheer cupcakes with vintage cupcake toppers and decorated everyone's favorite peanut butter cracker cookie with a candy-coated snowflake. For the cake, I baked my favorite chocolaty devil's food cake and coated the sides and tops in coconut, then topped it with an old-fashioned paper angel tree topper my grandma gave me years ago.

No matter what, the Christmas table is created by incorporating family tradition, whether it's décor, activities or actual family recipes. My recipes should help you do just that.

SETTING THE TABLE

While rifling through my attic for table props, I noticed the impressive collection of assorted vintage holiday boxes I've gathered over the years—boxes ranging from ornaments, tinsel and garlands, to Christmas lights and actual gift boxes. I scooped them up while contemplating how I could include them in my display. I collected a few other pieces that had reds or whites and carried them all downstairs to begin setting up my table. I pulled a few of my favorite Christmas decorations out that I thought would round out my table: vintage Santa mugs, an old toy fire truck, a decorative drum, a few bottlebrush trees and of course, a few of my vintage elves. Try to find table decor from your own stashed-away holiday boxes—vintage or not. If it's meaningful to you, you can use it on your dessert table.

NORTH POLE BAKERY DESSERTS

- ♥ Let It Snow Coconut Cake
- ♥ North Pole Cupcakes
- ♥ Snowflake Hockey Pucks
- ♥ Candy Cane Marshmallows

- ♥ First Noel Fudge
- ♥ Reindeer Chow
- ♥ Snowball Cookies
- ♥ Jolly Gingerbread Man Cookies
- ♥ Reindeer Cookies

- ♥ Santa Hat Cookies
- ♥ Snowflake Cookies
- ♥ Snowman Cookies
- ♥ Angel Cookies

Let It Snow Coconut Cake

SNOWY WHITE BUTTERCREAM FROSTING AND MOUNDS OF SWEETENED COCONUT FLAKES
HIDE THIS CAKE'S INNER BEAUTY. INSIDE ARE MOIST CHOCOLATY CAKE LAYERS FILLED
WITH EVEN MORE BUTTERCREAM. IT MAKES A PERFECT WINTER WONDERLAND
CENTERPIECE ON ANY DESSERT TABLE.

MAKES ONE 6-INCH (15 CM) AND 8-INCH (20.5 CM) TIERED CAKE

INGREDIENTS

COOKING SPRAY OR CRISCO OR
BUTTER PLUS FLOUR, FOR PANS

2 (18.25-OUNCE [517 G]) BOXES
DUNCAN HINES CHOCOLATE CAKE MIX

2 (3.4-OUNCE [110 G]) BOXES JELL-O
INSTANT PUDDING AND PIE FILLING,
DRY

2 CUPS (475 ML) WATER

⅔ CUP (157 ML) OIL

8 LARGE EGGS

2 BATCHES BUTTERCREAM FROSTING
(PAGE 10)

1 (14-OUNCE [400 G]) PACKAGE
SWEETENED COCONUT FLAKES

YOU WILL NEED

2 (8 × 2-INCH [20.5 × 5 CM]) AND
2 (6 × 2-INCH [15 × 5 CM]) ROUND
NONSTICK CAKE PANS

CAKE CUTTER OR LONG, SERRATED
KNIFE

2 ROUND CARDBOARD OR PLASTIC
CAKE BOARDS

OFFSET ANGLED SPATULA

5 (¼-INCH (6 MM]-THICK) DOWELS OR
THICK PLASTIC STRAWS

LARGE FLAT SPATULA

CAKE DECORATING TURNTABLE

LARGE DECORATING SPATULA

DIRECTIONS FOR THE CAKE:

1. Preheat the oven to 350°F (180°C). Coat the 8-inch (20.5 cm) and 6-inch (15 cm) round nonstick cake pans with cooking spray or grease and flour the pans, tapping out the excess flour. Set the prepared pans aside.

2. In a large bowl, and using an electric stand mixer fitted with a paddle attachment, beat the cake mix, pudding mix, water, oil and eggs on medium speed for 2 to 3 minutes, or until well blended. Scrape the sides of the bowl and mix again until all the ingredients are incorporated.

3. Pour batter into the prepared cake pans, filling each one approximately three-quarters full.

4. Place the pans in the preheated oven, on the middle rack. Bake the 6-inch (15 cm) cakes for 25 to 30 minutes, and the 8-inch (20.5 cm) cakes for 30 to 35 minutes, or until a toothpick inserted into the center comes out clean.

5. Remove the pans from the oven and place on wire cooling racks for 25 to 30 minutes. Run a knife around the edges of the cakes, flip the pans over and gently extract the cakes. Return the cakes to the wire racks and finish cooling completely before frosting and decorating. After the layers are cooled, freeze or refrigerate the cakes for 1 hour before decorating to reduce crumbs and make for a smoother icing process.

6. Meanwhile, make the two batches of buttercream frosting, adding one-half bag of the coconut flakes while mixing.

TO ASSEMBLE AND DECORATE THE CAKE

1. Before decorating, trim the crowns from the cake tops with a cake cutter or long, serrated knife so they are flat and even.

2. Place one of the 8-inch (20.5 cm) cakes on a cake board. Using the angled cake spatula, spread about ½ cup (120 ml) of frosting evenly across the top of the cake layer. Place the second 8-inch (20.5 cm) cake on top of the first, with the cut side on the bottom. Use the angled cake spatula to cover the cake completely with a very thin layer of icing (or crumb coat) to help reduce the amount of crumbs in the final coat of icing. Set the two-tiered 8-inch (20.5 cm) cake aside.

3. Repeat this process with the 6-inch (15 cm) cake layers, using another ½ cup (120 ml) of buttercream between the layers, and icing the sides and top of the cake. Once the same process has been completed on the 6-inch (15 cm) cake layers, allow them to dry for 1 hour, or until the icing crusts.

4. Create supports for the smaller cake to sit atop the larger cake by placing the dowels into the top of the 8-inch (20.5 cm) cake. Insert the first dowel into the cake and use a pen to mark the dowel at the point where it just comes to the top of the cake. Remove the dowel and cut it at that mark. Cut three to four additional dowels or straws to the same length and place them in a circle, approximately 2 inches (5 cm) from the center of the cake, and evenly spaced. Using a large flat spatula, carefully center and place the 6-inch (15 cm) tier on top of the 8-inch (20.5 cm) cake tier.

5. Place the cake on a rotating cake turntable. Starting at the top of the cake, and using a large decorating spatula, frost the top of the cake. Continue with the sides of both tiers, icing it until you reach the bottom. Lightly press the remaining coconut on top and sides of cake.

North Pole Cupcakes

SANTA WILL BE THRILLED WHEN HE SEES THESE ADORABLE CUPCAKES ON CHRISTMAS EVE, BUT HE'LL NEVER EXPECT WHAT'S BURIED INSIDE WHEN HE TAKES HIS FIRST BITE. UNDERNEATH A PILE OF BUTTERCREAM FROSTING IS A GINGERSNAP COOKIE HIDDEN DEEP INSIDE THE ULTRA-MOIST VANILLA CUPCAKE.

MAKES 24 STANDARD CUPCAKES

INGREDIENTS

1 (12-OUNCE [340 G]) PACKAGE GREEN CANDY MELTS

24 CANDY CANE STICKS

24 GINGERSNAP COOKIES

1 (18.25-OUNCE [517 G]) BOX DUNCAN HINES FRENCH VANILLA CAKE MIX

1 (3.4-OUNCE [110 G]) BOX JELL-O FRENCH VANILLA INSTANT PUDDING AND PIE FILLING, DRY

1 CUP (235 ML) WATER

⅓ CUP (80 ML) OIL

4 LARGE EGGS

1 BATCH BUTTERCREAM FROSTING (PAGE 10)

24 RED GUMBALLS

YOU WILL NEED

PLASTIC CANDY MOLD FOR SMALL RECTANGULAR DECORATIONS

COOKIE SCOOP

4 DISPOSABLE PASTRY BAGS

#1 WILTON DECORATING TIP

#1M WILTON DECORATING TIP

#4 WILTON DECORATING TIP

1 WILTON COUPLER

WAXED PAPER

2 STANDARD-SIZE CUPCAKE TRAYS

24 STANDARD PAPER CUPCAKE LINERS

DIRECTIONS

1. Melt the green candy melts in a microwave-safe bowl in 30-second increments at 40% power for about 1½ minutes, stirring as needed until smooth. Pour melted candy in disposable pastry bag and trim tip with scissors. Fill the candy mold with the melted candy and chill until set, about 30 minutes. Remove the candies from the mold. When dry, use a dab of melted candy to adhere one sign to each of the peppermint sticks.

2. With a pastry bag filled with a small amount of buttercream frosting, and fitted with Wilton decorating tip #1, write North Pole on each piece of candy. Set aside for about 1 hour on a sheet of waxed paper.

3. Preheat the oven to 350°F (180°C). Line the cupcake trays with paper cupcake liners. Place one gingersnap cookie in the bottom of each liner. Set the prepared pans aside.

4. In a large bowl, and using an electric stand mixer fitted with a paddle attachment, beat the cake mix, pudding mix, water, oil and eggs on medium speed for 2 to 3 minutes, or until well blended. Scrape down the sides of the bowl, and mix again until all the ingredients are incorporated.

5. Using a cookie scoop, fill each paper liner with batter to fill the liner about two-thirds full, dividing evenly between the cupcake trays.

6. Bake the cupcakes for 18 to 20 minutes, or until a toothpick inserted into the center comes out clean, or the tops spring back when lightly touched. Remove the cupcakes from the oven and place the trays on wire cooling racks for 5 minutes. Take the cupcakes out of the trays and allow them to cool completely on the wire racks before decorating.

7. Meanwhile, make the one batch of buttercream frosting.

8. Place the #1M Wilton decorating tip inside the pastry bag (no need to use a coupler) and fill with frosting.

9. To decorate the cupcakes, hold the pastry bag in an upright position, starting from the outer circle, squeeze the bag while turning clockwise, to make a large swirly rosette. Insert one peppermint stick North Pole sign on the top of each cupcake. Using a pastry bag fitted with the #4 decorating tip, dot the top of each peppermint stick with white frosting and fasten one red gumball to each.

Holiday Cheer Mini Cupcakes

LIKE NEWLY FALLEN SNOW, THESE BITE-SIZE CUPCAKES ARE PILED HIGH WITH PEPPERMINT FROSTING, AND GLISTENING WITH JUST ENOUGH SWEET SUGAR CRYSTALS TO MAKE YOU THINK YOU LANDED AT THE NORTH POLE.

MAKES 48 MINI CUPCAKES

INGREDIENTS

1 (18.25-OUNCE [517 G]) BOX DUNCAN HINES WHITE CAKE MIX

1 (3.4-OUNCE [110 G]) BOX JELL-O VANILLA INSTANT PUDDING AND PIE FILLING, DRY

1 CUP (235 ML) WATER

⅓ CUP (80 ML) OIL

4 LARGE EGGS

1 TEASPOON PEPPERMINT EXTRACT

1 BATCH BUTTERCREAM FROSTING (PAGE 10)

WHITE SUGAR CRYSTALS

YOU WILL NEED

2 MINI CUPCAKE TRAYS

48 MINI PAPER CUPCAKE LINERS

COOKIE SCOOP

LARGE PASTRY BAG

#1A WILTON DECORATING TIP

48 SMALL CHRISTMAS TREE CAKE TOPPERS/CUPCAKE PICKS

DIRECTIONS

1. Preheat the oven to 350°F (180°C). Line the mini cupcake trays with paper liners. Set the prepared trays aside.

2. In a large bowl, and using an electric stand mixer fitted with a paddle attachment, beat the cake mix, pudding mix, water, oil, eggs and ½ teaspoon of the peppermint extract on medium speed for 2 to 3 minutes, or until well blended. Scrape the sides of the bowl and mix again until all the ingredients are incorporated.

3. Using a cookie scoop, fill each paper liner with batter to fill the liner about two-thirds full, dividing evenly between the cupcake trays.

4. Bake the cupcakes for 10-13 minutes, or until a toothpick inserted into the center comes out clean or the tops spring back when lightly touched. Remove the cupcakes from the oven and place the trays on wire cooling racks for 5 minutes. Take the cupcakes out of the trays and allow them to cool completely on the wire racks before decorating.

5. Meanwhile, make the one batch of buttercream frosting, adding the remaining ½ teaspoon of peppermint extract during mixing. Place the #1A Wilton decorating tip inside the pastry bag (no need to use a coupler) and fill with frosting.

6. To decorate the cupcakes, hold the pastry bag in an upright position, squeeze the bag while turning clockwise, to make a large swirl. No need to be perfect! Place the white sugar crystals in a shallow bowl. Dip the cupcakes upside down in the sugar, covering the frosting completely. Place a green Christmas tree topper on top.

Snowflake Hockey Pucks

WITH ALL THE SNOW-WHITE DESSERTS ON THE CHRISTMAS TABLE, THESE BRIGHT RED HOCKEY PUCKS MAKE THE TABLE POP WITH HOLIDAY COLOR. WAIT TILL YOU TAKE A BITE—THERE'S A SWEET AND SALTY PEANUT BUTTER CENTER INSIDE.

MAKES 17 COOKIES

INGREDIENTS

1 PACKAGE (SLEEVE OF 34) RITZ CRACKERS

1 CUP (260 G) SMOOTH PEANUT BUTTER (I USE JIF)

1 (12-OUNCE [340 G]) PACKAGE WHITE CANDY MELTS

3 (12-OUNCE [340 G]) PACKAGES RED CANDY MELTS

YOU WILL NEED

DISPOSABLE PASTRY BAG

WAXED PAPER

DIRECTIONS

1. Melt the candy melts in separate microwave-safe bowls in 30-second increments at 40% power for about 2 to 3 minutes, stirring as needed until smooth. Set aside the white melted candy.

2. Turn the Ritz crackers upside down on a cookie sheet. Fill the pastry bag with peanut butter and trim the tip with scissors. Pipe a dollop of peanut butter on half the crackers. Place the remaining crackers on top to make sandwiches.

3. Using a fork, dip the crackers into the melted red candy. Place on waxed paper and let dry.

4. Pour the remaining melted white candy into a pastry bag and trim a small tip with scissors. Draw a snowflake on each cookie with white candy.

Candy Cane Marshmallows

JUST LIKE GREAT BIG SNOWBALLS, THESE JUMBO PUFFY MARSHMALLOWS ARE DIPPED IN CHOCOLATE AND ROLLED IN CRUSHED CANDY CANES WITH A PERFECTLY SIZED CANDY CANE HANDLE. THESE SWEET MINTY TREATS ARE ADORABLE HUNG FROM A CUP OF HOT COCOA ON A COLD WINTER'S DAY.

MAKES 24 TREATS

INGREDIENTS

24 JUMBO MARSHMALLOWS

1 (12-OUNCE [340 G]) PACKAGE RED CANDY MELTS

24 MINI CANDY CANES

2 CUPS CRUSHED CANDY CANES

YOU WILL NEED

WAXED PAPER

DIRECTIONS

1. Insert the candy canes into the marshmallows and set aside.

2. Melt the red candy melts in a microwave-safe bowl in 30-second increments at 40% power for about 1½ minutes, stirring as needed until smooth.

3. Dip the marshmallows two-thirds into the melted candy. They don't have to be perfect.

4. Sprinkle the crushed candy canes on the candy while still wet, making sure to let some red candy show through (eat within hours, or candy canes become sticky). Place on waxed paper to dry.

First Noel Fudge

WHO DOESN'T LOVE FUDGE FOR CHRISTMAS? MADE WITH SEMISWEET CHOCOLATE
AND MARSHMALLOW CREAM, IT'S THE FUDGE THEY ALL REMEMBER.

Note: *The timing and/or temperature is crucial for good results in this fudge recipe. I can't stress this enough. Set a timer for exactly 4 minutes.*
If you have a candy thermometer, it's still a good idea to set your timer for 4 minutes for the creamiest and best-tasting fudge!

MAKES 30 PIECES

INGREDIENTS

3 CUPS (600 G) GRANULATED SUGAR

¾ CUP (170 G) BUTTER OR MARGARINE

1 (5-OUNCE [148 ML]) CAN
EVAPORATED MILK (NOT SWEETENED
CONDENSED MILK)

3 (4-OUNCE [113 G]) PACKAGES
BAKER'S SEMISWEET BAKING
CHOCOLATE BARS

1 (7-OUNCE [798 G]) JAR JET-PUFFED
MARSHMALLOW CREME

1 TEASPOON PURE VANILLA EXTRACT

1 CUP CHOPPED CANDY CANES

YOU WILL NEED

9 × 13-INCH (23 × 33 CM) BAKING PAN
OR CASSEROLE DISH

CANDY THERMOMETER

1-INCH (2.5 CM) ROUND
COOKIE CUTTER

30 MINI PAPER CUPCAKE LINERS

DIRECTIONS

1. Lightly oil or spray the 9 × 13-inch (23 × 33 cm) baking pan with vegetable spray.

2. In a 3-quart (3.3L) saucepan over medium heat, mix the sugar, butter, and evaporated milk, stirring constantly until the mixture comes to a full rolling boil.

3. Clip the candy thermometer to the side of the pan, and continue cooking for exactly 4 minutes, or until the temperature reaches exactly 234°F (113°C), stirring constantly. Remove from the heat.

4. Stir in the chocolates and marshmallow creme, and stir until completely melted. Add the vanilla and stir again.

5. Pour the fudge into the prepared 9 × 13-inch (23 × 33 cm) pan, spreading evenly. Sprinkle the chopped candy canes on top, and let cool completely before cutting.

6. Using a 1-inch (2.5 cm) round cookie cutter, cut out fudge and place in mini baking cups to serve.

Rice Krispie Christmas Trees

JUST LIKE GOING OUT ON A COLD WINTER MORNING TO CUT DOWN A FRESH CHRISTMAS TREE,
THESE RICE KRISPIE TREES ARE CUT OUT WITH COOKIE CUTTERS AND PLANTED IN
A REESE'S PEANUT BUTTER CUP, THEN COVERED IN GREEN SPINKLES AND TOPPED
WITH A SINGLE CANDY STAR TO RESEMBLE A REAL TREE.

MAKES 15 TO 18 TREATS

INGREDIENTS

VEGETABLE SPRAY

3 TABLESPOONS (42 G) BUTTER OR MARGARINE

1 (10-OUNCE [280 G]) PACKAGE MINI MARSHMALLOWS (4 CUPS)

AMERICOLOR GREEN SOFT GEL PASTE COLOR

6 CUPS (150 G) RICE KRISPIES CEREAL

2 CUPS GREEN SPRINKLES

15 TO 18 MINIATURE REESE'S PEANUT BUTTER CUPS, UNWRAPPED

½ CUP (104 G) GREEN CANDY MELTS

15 TO 18 TEENY YELLOW STAR CANDY SPRINKLE DECORATIONS

YOU WILL NEED

9 × 13-INCH (23 × 33 CM) BAKING PAN OR CASSEROLE DISH

TRIANGLE COOKIE CUTTER

WAXED PAPER

DIRECTIONS

1. Lightly oil or spray the 9 × 13-inch (23 × 33 cm) baking pan with vegetable spray.

2. In a large saucepan over low heat, melt the butter or. Add the marshmallows and stir until melted and smooth. Remove the pan from the heat and add green food coloring to get the desired shade of green.

3. Add the Rice Krispies and stir until completely coated. Pat into the prepared baking pan and let cool completely to set. Once set, cut out tree shapes using the triangle cookie cutter.

4. Dip the Rice Krispie treats in the green sprinkles and lay flat on waxed paper.

5. Melt the green candy melts in a microwave-safe bowl in 30-second increments at 40% power for about 1 minute, stirring as needed until smooth.

6. Use a dab of melted candy to adhere the tree to the top of the peanut butter cup.

7. Add a yellow star sprinkle to the top of the tree with a spot of melted candy, and voilà—Rice Krispie trees!

Reindeer Chow

SANTA'S REINDEER NEED TO EAT WELL TO KEEP UP THEIR STRENGTH, ESPECIALLY IF THEY'RE DELIVERING PRESENTS ON CHRISTMAS EVE. TALK ABOUT EASY: THESE BITE-SIZE MORSELS ARE COATED WITH PEANUT BUTTER AND CHOCOLATY GOODNESS AND DUSTED WITH CONFECTIONERS' SUGAR SNOW FOR JUST THE RIGHT TOUCH.

MAKES 15 TO 18 TREATS

INGREDIENTS

12 CUPS (372 G) CHEX CEREAL

¾ CUP (170 G) BUTTER OR MARGARINE

1½ CUPS (262 G) SEMISWEET CHOCOLATE CHIPS

1½ CUPS (390 G) PEANUT BUTTER (I USE JIF)

3 CUPS (375 G) CONFECTIONERS' SUGAR

YOU WILL NEED

EXTRA-LARGE MIXING BOWL

LARGE BROWN PAPER BAG

DIRECTIONS

1. Pour the Chex cereal in a large bowl and set aside.

2. In a 3-quart (3.3L) saucepan over medium heat, melt the butter, chocolate chips and peanut butter until smooth. Pour over the cereal and mix together until the cereal is completely coated.

3. Place 1 cup (125 g) of confectioners' sugar in a large brown paper bag. Add the cereal mixture and shake well to coat. Add a second cup (125 g) of confectioners' sugar and toss again. Add the remaining 1 cup (125 g) of confectioners' sugar and shake to coat completely.

4. Store in an open container until ready to serve.

Snowball Cookies

SNOW WHITE SNOWBALL COOKIES—ALSO KNOWN AS PECAN BUTTERBALLS—ARE SO BUTTERY AND TENDER, THEY MELT IN YOUR MOUTH.

INGREDIENTS

1 CUP (225 G) BUTTER, AT ROOM TEMPERATURE (2 STICKS)

½ CUP (125 G) CONFECTIONERS' SUGAR

1 TEASPOON PURE VANILLA EXTRACT

2 TEASPOONS WATER

2¼ CUPS (181 G) ALL-PURPOSE FLOUR

½ TEASPOON SALT

¾ CUP (75 G) WALNUTS OR PECANS, CHOPPED

1 CUP (250 G) CONFECTIONERS' SUGAR, FOR ROLLING

YOU WILL NEED

2 NONSTICK COOKIE SHEETS

SMALL COOKIE SCOOP OR TABLESPOON

DIRECTIONS

1. Preheat the oven to 400°F (204°C).

2. In a large mixing bowl, and using an electric mixer on medium speed with the paddle attachment, or with a large bowl and mixing spoon, beat the butter and the confectioners' sugar until creamy. Add the vanilla and water and continue beating until the batter is nice and smooth, scraping the bowl with a rubber spatula as needed. Add the flour, salt and chopped nuts and mix once more until the ingredients are incorporated.

3. Using a cookie scoop, measure evenly sized balls and place on ungreased cookie sheets.

4. Bake for 8 to 10 minutes, or until the cookies are just beginning to brown.

5. Remove the cookies from the oven and as soon as they are cool enough to handle, roll in the confectioners' sugar. Set aside to cool, then roll in the confectioners' sugar again.

Jolly
Gingerbread Man Cookies

BETTER-THAN-SCRATCH COOKIES, THESE GINGERBREAD MEN
ARE AS EASY AS THEY ARE DELICIOUS. I START OUT WITH A BOXED
GINGERBREAD CAKE MIX, ADD A FEW INGREDIENTS, AND BEFORE YOU KNOW IT,
SPICY GINGERBREAD MEN ARE JUMPING OUT OF THE OVEN
AND TAKING OVER THE KITCHEN.

MAKES 15 TO 18 COOKIES

INGREDIENTS

1 BOX GINGERBREAD CAKE MIX

¼ CUP (60 ML) HOT WATER

2 TABLESPOONS (16 G) ALL-PURPOSE
FLOUR

2 TABLESPOONS (28 G) BUTTER OR
MARGARINE

½ CUP (120 ML) BUTTERCREAM
FROSTING (PAGE 10)

YOU WILL NEED

2 NONSTICK COOKIE SHEETS

DISPOSABLE PASTRY BAG

#4 WILTON DECORATING TIP

WILTON COUPLER

DIRECTIONS

1. In a large mixing bowl, and using an electric mixer on medium speed with the paddle attachment, mix all the ingredients until a medium consistency dough forms, scraping the bowl with a rubber spatula as needed.

2. Divide the dough into 2 equal-size balls. Wrap each ball in a piece of plastic wrap and press down to form 1-inch (2.5 cm)-thick disks. Refrigerate for at least 1 hour before rolling.

3. Preheat the oven to 375°F (190°C).

4. Roll out the dough on a lightly floured flat work surface to about ¼-inch (6 mm) thickness, using additional flour as necessary to prevent sticking. Cut out gingerbread man cookie shapes and carefully transfer with a spatula to a nonstick baking sheet, placing the cookies about ¾ inch (2 cm) apart. Continue rolling out the gathered scraps and the remaining disk until all the dough has been used.

5. Bake one sheet at a time in the middle of the oven for about 8 minutes, or until the edges are firm. Allow the cookies to rest for 2 minutes on the baking sheet before transferring to a wire rack to cool completely before decorating.

6. To decorate the gingerbread men, using a pastry bag filled with white buttercream and fitted with a #4 decorating tip, pipe eyes, nose, mouth, three buttons and squiggly zigzags on arms and legs.

North Pole Bakery Jenny Cookies

IF YOU'RE PLANNING ON MAKING ALL FIVE SUGAR COOKIES ON THE CHRISTMAS TABLE AS THEY'RE PICTURED, YOU'LL NEED ONE BATCH OF BUTTERCREAM FROSTING, PREPARED AS DIRECTED ON PAGE 10.

IT'LL SAVE YOU TIME IF YOU COLOR THE BUTTERCREAM AND FILL EACH PASTRY BAG BEFORE YOU BEGIN DECORATING. USE DISPOSABLE PASTRY BAGS AND THROW THEM AWAY WHEN YOU'RE DONE. YOU'LL BE USING MORE WHITE FROSTING THAN ANY OTHER COLOR, AND JUST A LITTLE LESS OF THE RED AND BROWN FROSTING, SO MAKE SURE YOU FILL THOSE PASTRY BAGS FIRST. THEN TINT A VERY SMALL AMOUNT OF BUTTERCREAM WITH ORANGE, MINT GREEN AND BLACK. ATTACH WILTON DECORATING TIPS AND COUPLERS TO EACH OF THE PASTRY BAGS AND FILL WITH FROSTING. IF YOU DON'T HAVE ENOUGH #4 AND #18 WILTON DECORATING TIPS FOR ALL THE BAGS, JUST CHANGE THEM OUT, WASH THEM AND PUT THEM IN ANOTHER BAG (USING COUPLERS MAKES CHANGING TIPS SO EASY). YOU'LL MAKE ONE BATCH OF SUGAR COOKIE DOUGH AND USE IT FOR ALL THE COOKIE SHAPES. SEE PAGE 12 FOR THE COOKIE INGREDIENTS AND DIRECTIONS.

MAKES ABOUT 24 COOKIES

YOU WILL NEED

ROLLING PIN
2 NONSTICK COOKIE SHEETS
COOKIE SPATULA
REINDEER COOKIE CUTTER
SANTA HAT COOKIE CUTTER
SNOWFLAKE COOKIE CUTTER
SNOWMAN COOKIE CUTTER
ANGEL COOKIE CUTTER
6 DISPOSABLE PASTRY BAGS
6 #4 WILTON DECORATING TIPS
1 #18 WILTON DECORATING TIP
6 WILTON COUPLERS
AMERICOLOR SOFT GEL PASTE
COLORS; RED, BROWN, ORANGE, MINT
GREEN AND BLACK
GOLD SUGAR CRYSTALS

Reindeer Cookies

INGREDIENTS

BROWN BUTTERCREAM
WHITE BUTTERCREAM
RED BUTTERCREAM

To decorate the reindeer cookies, place brown buttercream frosting in a pastry bag fitted with a #4 Wilton decorating tip. Outline the entire reindeer, making sure to add antlers. Fill in with brown frosting, running it horizontally from one edge of the outlines to the other, until the body is filled in. Using a pastry bag with red frosting and #4 tip, give the reindeer a red nose. Give him four or five spots using the bag with white frosting and #4 tip.

(continued)

Santa Hat Cookies

INGREDIENTS

RED BUTTERCREAM

WHITE BUTTERCREAM

To decorate the Santa hat cookies, use the pastry bag filled with red frosting and fitted with a #4 Wilton decorating tip. Begin by outlining the triangle portion of his hat first, then fill it in with red frosting, running it horizontally from one edge of the outlines to the other, until it's filled in. Using the pastry bag with white frosting and #18 Wilton decorating tip, fill in the cuff of the hat with fluffy, billowy frosting using a swirled hand motion. Add a white frosting swirled rosette to the tip of his hat.

Snowflake Cookies

INGREDIENTS

WHITE BUTTERCREAM

RED BUTTERCREAM

To decorate the snowflake cookies, use the pastry bag filled with white frosting, and fitted with a #18 Wilton decorating tip. Beginning at the end of each snowflake point, fill in the cookie moving toward the center, creating white swirly zigzags. Repeat each arm of the snowflake until you meet in the center. Use the pastry bag filled with red buttercream and a #4 Wilton tip to finish drawing the arms of the snowflake.

Snowman Cookies

INGREDIENTS

WHITE BUTTERCREAM

RED BUTTERCREAM

ORANGE BUTTERCREAM

MINT GREEN BUTTERCREAM

BLACK BUTTERCREAM

To decorate the snowman cookies, use the pastry bag filled with white frosting and fitted with a #4 Wilton decorating tip. Begin by outlining his body of snowballs first, avoiding his hat and carrot nose. Fill in his body with white frosting, running it horizontally from one edge of the outlines to the other, until it is completely filled in. Using the pastry bag with red frosting and #4 Wilton decorating tip, outline and fill in his hat, then finish his hat by using the bag with white buttercream to make polka dots. Using the pastry bags with mint green and orange frosting and #4 tips, draw a mint green scarf around his neck, and give him an orange carrot nose. Draw on one black eye with pastry bag filled with black buttercream.

Angel Cookies

INGREDIENTS

WHITE BUTTERCREAM

GOLD SUGAR CRYSTALS

To decorate the angel cookies, use the pastry bag filled with white frosting, and fitted with a #4 Wilton decorating tip. Begin by outlining both the angle's wings and halo first. Fill in the wings and halo with frosting, then turn upside down in a plate of gold sugar crystals to adhere to the frosting completely. Using the pastry bag with white frosting and #18 Wilton decorating tip, fill in the angel's body with fluffy, billowy frosting in a swirly pattern.

Glossary

- **AmeriColor soft gel paste**: Gel food coloring. These pastes provide a more intense color without any change in taste.

- **Ateco**: Ateco cake decorating supplies are high-end, quality baking tools designed for commercial and home bakers alike.

- **Candy melt:** Candy melts are often recommended for easy candy-making or coating cake pops. They come in many colors and have a plain, vaguely milky flavor that serves as a base for additional flavorings. Many people make the mistake of thinking that these are chocolate, since they're recommended for candy making, but these melts are not chocolate. They're primarily made with a combination of sugar and vegetable fats, not cocoa butter. Candy melts are easy to use—just melt and dip—and they come in a wide variety of colors, which makes it easy to decorate with them and achieve many looks.

- **Candy mold:** Plastic trays with various cavities that shape melted candy when it cools and hardens.

- **Candy oil:** An edible oil used to color chocolate and other substances that would otherwise seize with a traditional soft gel paste (like food coloring). Candy oil is the ideal way to turn any white candy melt into whatever special color you want without altering the flavor.

- **Couplers**: A two-piece device that fits onto your decorating bag and holds the decorating tip in place. It's great when you want to change decorating tips without changing bags. The coupler base goes inside the cut bag to hold the tip in place, while the coupler ring twists around the base on the outside of the bag to attach the tip. Just twist off the ring to change tips.

- **Decorating bag:** Decorating bags are lightweight, flexible, reinforced for strength and can be reused. Decorating bags are made of either polyester or disposable plastic. They hold the icing and decorating tip so you can create a variety of decorations.

- **Decorating tips**: These small metal cones are shaped to produce various designs when icing is pressed through them. The size and shape of the opening on a decorating bag tip identifies the basic group or family to which the tip belongs and determines the type of decorations the tip will produce. Each tip has a number stamped in the tip itself.

- **Petal tips:** Realistic flower petals, dramatic ruffles, drapes, swags and bows. All tips work with standard bags and couplers, unless otherwise indicated.

- **Round tips:** Used for outlining details, filling and piping in areas, writing and printing messages, figure piping, dots, etc. These tips are smooth and round.

- **Star tips:** Star tips produce the most popular decorations—deeply grooved shells, stars, fleur-de-lis, rosettes and flowers.

- **Sixlets:** Small, round, candy-coated, multicolor, chocolate-flavored candy.

- **Wilton:** Wilton Enterprises, Inc. is an innovator in cake-decorating and candy-making products.

Acknowledgments

To my readers, I've poured my ideas, designs, recipes and love into this project. May this book spark your creative gene and inspire you to celebrate all of life's occasions both big and small.

A huge thank you to everyone at Page Street Publishing, including the wonderful team that made this book happen. Kara Baskin, Meg Baskis, Marissa Giambelluca, Meg Palmer and especially William Kiester, for turning my vision into a reality.

My agent, Coleen O'Shea. Thank you for leading me in the right direction and believing in this project from the beginning. Your guidance, advice and constant push to "get this done" is much appreciated.

Many thanks to Donna Diegel for your delightful editorial contribution. So many cross-country conversations searching for the perfect words to describe each and every dessert. Your words brought life to my recipes and wonderful direction for eager fans and future bakers.

My fantastic photographer and friend Kelly Bowie. You are talented beyond belief. There's no other person I'd rather have shared this experience with. Your humor and wit kept me going long after the point of exhaustion. Your gorgeous photography captured every detail and ounce of my design.

My brilliant florist Chelsea Dudder-Cox. Your talent amazes me. My dessert tables were brightened with your incredible creations. Thank you for your time, talent and floral flair.

Tori, you've had a huge impact on my work and success, for which I am so grateful. You took a chance on a small-town girl and granted an opportunity that challenged me to be the best I could be. Working with you has caused me to compete with myself to guarantee every dessert table I create is superior to the last.

Kennedi, who would have thought a gift of sugar cookies could lead to this? Thank you for seeing my talent and encouraging me to share it.

Naomi and Nazra, thank you for reassuring me that it's OK to go crazy when it comes to celebrating my children. You cheered my outrageous party ideas and believed in the memories made for my kids. Not every cookie creation can be the cutest ever, but your continual enthusiasm for my work means the world.

Scout, what would my nights be without our endless text exchanges surrounding our next event together or latest cake stand purchase? Thank you for being a second set of eyes when I've hit a creative roadblock and a voice of reason when I have 49 items in my eBay shopping cart. You've helped me grow my business and pushed me past my creative boundaries (Disco-Fiesta?). You are genuine, kind and stand out in a city of fakes. You are the real deal, my friend.

To my dearest friend, Abby. Thank you for your support, advice, love and enthusiasm. You inspire me daily as a mom and friend. I'm blessed by your friendship and the opportunity to do life with you. I can't imagine my days without you in them.

My beloved Grandma and Grandpa, thank you for teaching me that I was special enough to do anything I put my mind to. You filled me with confidence, love and beliefs that have molded the person I am today. You've inspired my love of baking, decorating and creating tradition and values for my family.

Thank you to my Aunt Susan, who always invited my creative baking into her kitchen when I was young, no matter how big of a disaster I made. It taught me to let my own children dump the sprinkles on, ice their own cookies and help scoop batter into the cupcake liner regardless of how messy. Life is precious. And there's no mess too big to clean up.

My sweet sister Emily. You've shown my family love beyond love. Thank you for your support and willingness to always help. You make me laugh and smile with your infectious sparkle. I'm so thankful God picked you for my sister.

Mom, I inherited your hustle. You've taught me how to work hard and to never give up. I've been far beyond blessed with your unconditional love. You make me believe anything is possible. And whether you believe it or not, my creativity really does come from you.

Ally and Hudson, I have strived to make your childhood memorable and magical, and in doing so, found a talent and passion I didn't know existed. You brighten my day and give my life so much meaning. I thank God every day for trusting me with the two of your lives.

Dan, you are my rock. My biggest fan, my forever love, and my best friend. My life is complete with you. Thank you for supporting my wild ideas and allowing me to truly live my dreams. I love you.

About the Author

JENNY KELLER, creator of the popular site www.jennycookies.com, is best known for the amazing dessert tables she bakes and creates for celebrity parties. Her one-of-a-kind desserts have been featured on people.com, HuffingtonPost.com and E! Online, as well as popular shows such as *E! News*, *Extra*, *Entertainment Tonight*, *The Insider* and *Tori & Dean, Home Sweet Hollywood*. Jenny lives in Seattle with her husband and two children.

Index

A

acorn donuts, 165
angel cookies, 218
apples
 autumn apple pies, 189
 nutty caramel apples, 187

B

baby bib cookies, 79
baby bliss cupcakes, 72
baby bottle cookies, 79
baby buggy cookies, 79
baby shower dessert table, 67–79
backdrops, 25
baking powder, 23
baking tips, 16, 19
banana
 mini banana split bites, 117
 pudding cups, 74
barn cookies, 141
birthday cake waffle cone cake pops, 120–121
brownies
 brownie ice cream sandwiches, 119
 brownie nests, 97
 brownie waffle bowl sundaes, 114
 don't feed the bears brownie pops, 168
bunny ear cookies, 100
bunny ear cupcakes, 91
buried treasure cupcakes, 153
butter, 23
buttercream frosting
 chocolate, 11
 recipe, 10
 tips for, 11

C

cake. see also cake pops
 acorn donuts, 165
 basic recipe, 15
 German chocolate harvest cake, 181–183
 green swirl ribbon cake, 83–84
 happy campers, 163–164
 hearts of gold rustic cake, 50–51
 ice cream cone cake, 105–106
 let it snow coconut cake, 200–201
 pink rose cake, 85–87
 red velvet ribbon cake, 130–131
 royal chocolate ruffle cake, 29–31
 shiver me timbers cake, 146–147
 swirled surprise cake, 69–71
 testing doneness of, 16

tips for baking and decorating, 16
yellow petal cake, 88–89
cake mix, 23
cake pans, preparation of, 16
cake pops, 20–22
 bibbidi bobbidi blue, 40
 birthday cake waffle cone, 120–121
 cannonball, 148
 cookies and cream, 132
 don't feed the bears brownie pops, 168
 filled with love, 55
 lemon bloom, 95
 pumpkin patch, 184
 strawberry sugar cone, 110
 tips, 22
cake topper, princess, 31
campground cookies, 167
campout dessert table, 159–177
 campground cookies, 167
 don't feed the bears brownie pops, 168
 great outdoors s'mores, 172
 happy campers cake, 163–164
 happy trails mix, 170
 Jenny cookies, 175–177
 kumbaya cupcakes, 171
 s'mores on a stick, 172
 table setting, 160
candy cane marshmallows, 207
candy melts, 23
candy molds, 19
candy oils, 23
cannonball cake pops, 148
canoe cookies, 176
captains parrot cookies, 156
caramel apples, nutty, 187
carrot cake
 pink rose cake, 85–87
carrot cookies, 100
cherry pies with lattice crust, mini, 137
chocolate
 brownie ice cream sandwiches, 119
 brownie nests, 97
 brownie waffle bowl sundaes, 114
 buried treasure cupcakes, 153
 buttercream frosting, 11
 cannonball cake pops, 148
 charming chocolate cupcake truffles, 35
 chocolate chip cookies, 167
 dilly bars, 116
 don't feed the bears brownie pops, 168
 first noel fudge, 208

German chocolate harvest cake, 181–183
great outdoors s'mores, 172
happy campers cake, 163–164
hydrangea flower pot cupcakes, 92
ice cream cone cake, 105–106
kumbaya cupcakes, 171
let it snow coconut cake, 200–201
royal chocolate ruffle cake, 29–31
shiver me timbers cake, 146–147
s'mores on a stick, 172
Christmas dessert table, 197–218
coconut
 let it snow coconut cake, 200–201
 pink vintage ruffle cupcakes, 52
color, use of, 25
confectioners' sugar, 23
cookie cutters, 14
cookies. see also Jenny cookies; sugar cookies
 campground, 167
 chocolate chip, 167
 dilly bars, 116
 gingerbread man, 214
 peanut butter, 150
 peanut butter bliss, 60
 pumpkin spice sandwich, 190
 rattles from Seattle, 75
 snowball, 213
 snowflake hockey pucks, 206
 strawberry sweetheart, 63
 tips for making, 14
cookies and cream cake pops, 132
cow cookies, 140
crossbones sugar cookies, 156
cupcakes
 baby bliss, 72
 baking tips, 19
 basic recipe, 18
 bunny ear, 91
 buried treasure, 153
 charming chocolate cupcake truffles, 35
 chocolate, 153, 171
 decorating tips, 19
 enchanted rose, 32
 farm fresh lemon, 129
 holiday cheer mini, 204
 hydrangea flower pot, 92
 kumbaya, 171
 North Pole, 203
 pink vintage ruffle, 52
 single scoop vanilla, 109
 whipped vanilla cream, 59

D

decorating tips, 16, 19
decorations, 24
dessert tables, 7
    campout, 159–177
    down on the farm, 125–141
    fall bounty, 179–195
    ice cream shop, 103–123
    love is sweet, 47–65
    North Pole bakery, 197–218
    princess tea party, 27–45
    shipwrecked, 143–157
    spring garden, 81–101
    tips for creating, 25
    vintage baby, 67–79
devil's food cake
    cannonball cake pops, 148
    charming chocolate cupcake truffles, 35
    cupcakes, 92
    happy campers cake, 163–164
    hydrangea flower pot cupcakes, 92
    ice cream cone cake, 105–106
    kumbaya cupcakes, 171
    royal chocolate ruffle cake, 29–31
    shiver me timbers cake, 146–147
dilly bars, 116
donuts, acorn, 165
down on the farm dessert table, 125–141
    cookies and cream cake pops, 132
    farm fresh lemon cupcakes, 129
    Jenny cookies, 139–141
    mini cherry pies with lattice crust, 137
    pigs in mud, 136
    red velvet ribbon cake, 130–131
    strawberry shortcakes in a jar, 135
    table setting, 126
Duncan Hines cake mixes, 16

E

eggs, 23
enchanted rose cupcakes, 32
equipment, 24
essential ingredients, 23
extracts, 23
eye patch Rice Krispie treats, 154

F

fall bounty dessert table, 179–195
    autumn apple pies, 189
    German chocolate harvest cake, 181–183
    Jenny cookies, 193–195
    nutty caramel apples, 187
    pumpkin patch cake pops, 184
    pumpkin spice sandwich cookies, 190
    Rice Krispie treat pumpkins, 186
    table setting, 180
fall leaf cookies, 194
farmhouse dessert table, 125–141
filled with love cake pops, 55
first noel fudge, 208
flour, 23
flower cookies, 99
flower Rice Krispie treats, 96
flowers, 25
food coloring, 23

G

garden carrot cookies, 100
German chocolate harvest cake, 181–183
gingerbread man cookies, 214
glass slipper sugar cookies, 44
gold doubloons PB cookies, 150
green swirl ribbon cake, 83–84

H

happy campers cake, 163–164
happy trails mix, 170
heart cookies, 44, 64
hearts of gold rustic cake, 50–51
holiday cheer mini cupcakes, 204
horse cookies, 139
hydrangea flower pot cupcakes, 92

I

ice cream cone cake, 105–106
ice cream cone cookies, 122
ice cream shop dessert table, 103–123
    birthday cake waffle cone cake pops, 120–121
    brownie ice cream sandwiches, 119
    brownie waffle bowl sundaes, 114
    dilly bars, 116
    ice cream cone cake, 105–106
    Jenny cookies, 122–123
    mini banana split bites, 117
    Rice Krispie treat ice cream bars, 113
    single scoop vanilla cupcakes, 109
    strawberry sugar cone cake pops, 110
    table setting, 104
ice cream sundae cookies, 123
ingredients, essential, 23

J

Jenny cookies
    campout, 175–177
    down on the farm, 139–141
    fall bounty, 193–195
    ice cream shop, 122–123
    love is sweet, 64
    North Pole baker, 217–218
    princess tea party, 43–44
    shipwrecked, 155–157
    spring garden, 99–101
    vintage baby, 77–79
Jenny Cookies blog, 6–7

K

kumbaya cupcakes, 171

L

lemon
    farm fresh lemon cupcakes, 129
    green swirl ribbon cake, 83–84
    lemon bloom cake pops, 95
let it snow coconut cake, 200–201
love is sweet dessert table, 47–65
    filled with love cake pops, 55
    hearts of gold rustic cake, 50–51
    Jenny cookies, 64

frosting
    buttercream, 10
    chocolate buttercream, 11
fudge, 208

    peanut butter bliss cookies, 60
    pink vintage ruffle cupcakes, 52
    strawberry sweetheart cookies, 63
    sweet as can be Rice Krispie treats, 56
    table setting, 48
    whipped vanilla cream cupcakes, 59

M

magic wand sugar cookies, 43
margarine, 23
marshmallow
    candy cane marshmallows, 207
    first noel fudge, 208
    great outdoors s'mores, 172
    marshmallow pillow pops, 39
    s'mores on a stick, 172
mini banana split bites, 117
mini ice cream cone cookies, 123
moose head cookies, 176

N

North Pole bakery dessert table, 197–218
    candy cane marshmallows, 207
    first noel fudge, 208
    gingerbread man cookies, 214
    holiday cheer mini cupcakes, 204
    Jenny cookies, 217–218
    let it snow coconut cake, 200–201
    North Pole cupcakes, 203
    reindeer chow, 212
    Rice Krispie Christmas trees, 211
    snowball cookies, 213
    snowflake hockey pucks, 206
    table setting, 198
North Pole cupcakes, 203
nutty caramel apples, 187

O

oil, 23
oven temperature, 16
owl cookies, 194

P

peanut butter
    buried treasure cupcakes, 153
    cookies, 150
    dilly bars, 116
    peanut butter bliss cookies, 60
    pigs in mud, 136
    Rice Krispie Christmas trees, 211
    snowflake hockey pucks, 206
    stork delivery bites, 73
pecan butterballs, 213
petal cake, 16
pies
    autumn apple pies, 189
    mini cherry pies with lattice crust, 137
pig cookies, 140
pigs in mud, 136
pinecone cookies, 175
pink and purple flower cookies, 99
pink rose cake, 85–87
pink vintage ruffle cupcakes, 52
pirate ship cookies, 156
pirate-themed dessert table, 143–157
planning, 25

popcorn
  she's going to pop corn, 76
princess tea party, 27–45
  bibbidi bobbidi blue cake pops, 40
  charming chocolate cupcake truffles, 35
  enchanted rose cupcakes, 32
  Jenny cookies, 43–44
  marshmallow pillow pops, 39
  royal chocolate ruffle cake, 29–31
  sparkle Rice Krispie wands, 36
  table setting, 28
princess tiara cookies, 44
puddings, 23
  banana pudding cups, 74
pumpkin
  pumpkin patch cake pops, 184
  pumpkin spice sandwich cookies, 190
  Rice Krispie treat pumpkins, 186
  sugar cookies, 193

R
rattle cookies, 77
rattles from Seattle, 75
red velvet
  filled with love cake pops, 55
  ribbon cake, 130–131
reindeer chow, 212
reindeer cookies, 217
ribbon cake, 16
  green swirl, 83–84
  red velvet, 130–131
rice cereal, 23
Rice Krispie treats
  eye patch, 154
  flower Rice Krispie treats, 96
  ice cream bars, 113
  ice cream cone cake, 105–106
  pumpkins, 186
  recipe, 23
  Rice Krispie Christmas trees, 211
  sparkle Rice Krispie wands, 36
  sweet as can be Rice Krispie treats, 56
  tips, 23
rooster cookies, 140
rose cake, 16, 85–87
rose cookies, 100
rose cupcakes, enchanted, 32
rose technique, 81–82
royal carriage cookies, 44
royal chocolate ruffle cake, 29–31
ruffle cake, 16
ruffle cupcakes, 52
rustic cake, 16

S
Santa hat cookies, 218
scalloped cake, 16
scarecrow cookies, 194
sheep cookies, 141
shipwrecked dessert table, 143–157
  buried treasure cupcakes, 153
  cannonball cake pops, 148
  eye patch Rice Krispie treats, 154
  gold doubloons PB cookies, 150
  Jenny cookies, 155–157
  shiver me timbers cake, 146–147
  table setting, 144

shiver me timbers cake, 146–147
single scoop vanilla cupcakes, 109
s'mores
  great outdoors s'mores, 172
  s'mores on a stick, 172
snacks
  happy trails mix, 170
  reindeer chow, 212
  she's going to pop corn, 76
snowball cookies, 213
snowflake cookies, 218
snowflake hockey pucks, 206
snowman cookies, 218
spackle cake, 16
spring garden dessert table, 81–101
  brownie nests, 97
  bunny ear cupcakes, 91
  flower Rice Krispie treats, 96
  green swirl ribbon cake, 83–84
  hydrangea flower pot cupcakes, 92
  Jenny cookies, 99–101
  lemon bloom cake pops, 95
  pink rose cake, 85–87
  table setting, 82
  yellow petal cake, 88–89
squirrel cookies, 176
stork delivery bites, 73
strawberry
  strawberry shortcakes in a jar, 135
  strawberry sugar cone cake pops, 110
  strawberry sweetheart cookies, 63
sugar, 23
sugar cookies, 12
  angel, 218
  baby bib, 79
  baby bottle, 79
  baby buggy, 79
  barn, 141
  bunny ear, 100
  canoe, 176
  captains parrot, 156
  carrot, 100
  cow, 140
  crossbones, 156
  fall leaf, 194
  flower, 99
  glass slipper, 44
  heart, 44, 64
  horse, 139
  ice cream cone, 122
  ice cream sundae, 123
  magic wand, 43
  mini ice cream cone, 123
  moose head, 176
  owl, 194
  pig, 140
  pinecone, 175
  pirate ship, 156
  princess tiara, 44
  pumpkin, 193
  rattle cookies, 77
  reindeer, 217
  rooster, 140
  royal carriage, 44
  Santa hat, 218
  scarecrow, 194
  sheep, 141

snowflake, 218
snowman, 218
squirrel, 176
swashbuckling sword, 155
teepee tent, 176
tractor, 140
treasure map, 156
wedding dress, 64
wheelbarrow, 194
yellow rose, 100
swashbuckling sword sugar cookies, 155
sweetheart dessert table, 47–65
swirled surprise cake, 69–71

T
teepee tent cookies, 176
theme, 25
tips
  cake pops, 22
  cake-baking and decorating, 16
  cookie-making, 14
  cupcake baking and decorating, 19
  dessert tables, 25
  Rice Krispie treats, 23
tools, 24
tractor cookies, 140
treasure map cookies, 156
truffles, charming chocolate cupcake, 35

V
vanilla, 23
  bibbidi bobbidi blue cake pops, 40
  buttercream frosting, 10
  enchanted rose cupcakes, 32
  North Pole cupcakes, 203
  single scoop vanilla cupcakes, 109
  whipped vanilla cream cupcakes, 59
vegetable shortening, 23
vintage baby dessert table, 67–79
  baby bliss cupcakes, 72
  bitty banana pudding cups, 74
  Jenny cookies, 77–79
  rattles from Seattle, 75
  she's going to pop corn, 76
  stork delivery bites, 73
  swirled surprise cake, 69–71
  table setting, 68

W
waffle cone cake pops, 120–121
wedding dress cookies, 64
wheelbarrow cookies, 194
whipped vanilla cream cupcakes, 59

Y
yellow petal cake, 88–89
yellow rose cookies, 100